The Word Pavilion
and
Selected Poems

Also by Christopher Middleton

CHRISTOPHER MIDDLETON

The Word Pavilion
and
Selected Poems

CARCANET

First published in Great Britain in 2001 by
Carcanet Press Limited
4th Floor, Conavon Court
12–16 Blackfriars Street
Manchester M3 5BQ

A CIP catalogue record for this book
is available from the British Library

ISBN 1 85754 512 5

The publisher acknowledges financial assistance
from the Arts Council of England

Printed and bound in England by SRP Ltd, Exeter

Acknowledgements for The Word Pavilion

Grateful acknowledgement is made to the editors of those reviews in which some of these poems first appeared; *Agenda*, *Babel* (Germany), *Grand Street*, *Literary Imagination*, *The London Review of Books*, *The New Yorker*, *Oasis*, *Partisan Review*, *P.N. Review*, *Poetry Kanto* (Japan), *Riversedge*, *Shearsman*.

Contents

THE WORD PAVILION

1

2

SELECTED POEMS

The Word Pavilion

1

Children's Corner

This music disappears into itself
– before you look, listen,
hear it sweep the sky
clean of soot, clean of stars, even.

Still, there it is, now domestic:
humming in her room below the roof
she services herself – a cake of soap,
a china jug, a bowl of water;

And scrub she must her skin –
a breast, a shoulder, carry, shaken forward,
chords of hair, coppery, unfolding.

She opens up the skylight – dare you look?
Circling now her mountaintop the witch, hallo,
star after star she taps back in, like new.

Lines for Jennifer

Ballerina oracle on a barstool,
You told me tonight of the foxes,
They are not extinct, but audible,
So your mother opens at nightfall
Her window and hears them bark,
And listens in late Spring to the chat,
Yellow-breasted, warbling, to the tiptoe
Scuffle of a coon, to the chirrup of her young –
A fine tale you told me, innocent,
Your country spangled with rivers
Pales in comparison, ballerina, even then,
With a daydream of yours, there on the barstool –
All your people, come through the hoop,
Reconvene, inexplicably remembered
In the bubble of time you sit bewitched in,
Now they tell how it was, ask if at all
In thought, in gesture, you resemble them,
Tell how memory smoke smells of apricot,
Colours of an old quilt, a lake in a wooded coomb
Perk up and shimmer in company with a mind,
And prompt as bell chimes constellating their days
They mimic ancient rages and Who Fought Whom,
Who starved, who wandered away for ever,
Show how strings of coincidence bring us here
With all our trouble, growing, to be alive,
Them, too, whispering of evils they resisted,
How to shine as long as you are alive,
Them, sharing your features, our secret
Transparent in their round, slow dance –
So they drink up the outline, liquid, of our exile.

Aladagh Mountain Sketches

1

The old Turk joined his two sheep near sundown,
Sat on a tree root, spoke now and then:
Tukurruk tukurruk. The sheep spoke back,
Not as sheep to sheep but *tukurruk tukurruk*,
The right way for a sheep to speak to a man.

2

All day since dawn in the blazing sun
And hauling what he has to haul,
Logs and apricots, hay and men,
Serene when he drinks, happy trotting,
The donkey brays a bit near nightfall.
When he brays, hold on to your hat,
His heaven is near, might sweep you in.

3

There was this bird suddenly with a trill
Delineating all the apple trees,
A trill like a whisker, the whisker bird;
And after this, the high call of the muezzin,
More whisker; the tractor, whisker; the apples,
Orchard whiskers, globular and green.

The wrinkled cloven features of the rock
Outcrops hereabouts, and this granny's:
Tenderly she gestured beside her –
On the road shoulder, at last gasp, her sheep.
But it can't die in the trunk like a hostage,
Can it? So we drove on, but granny
Who tutored sheep through misty generations,
From lamb's first leap to milking, to wool,
Each a silken pocket, full of foibles,
We left her looking back down the empty road.

5

"Life is hard, still harder when you're dumb" –
But they aren't, in the one-room stone and plaster
Huts, the graceful girls, headscarf knotted right,
In clean clothes, the mother with a scalded foot,
Taking the pain. They all sweat it out, him too,
Dawn to dusk, among the white beans, baba,
Granite face, who talks a streak.

6

Where from, the slender fingers?
With a carving knife she hacks
The block of snow somebody carried
Down the mountain. Just look,
How the slender fingers dip a piece
In the mound of sugar and establish it
Between tongue and teeth. In the town,
Wintertime . . . but it's far off.
Up here, we make do with snow cream.

Stone on stone, four walls rose
And a cupola was rounded;
A low portal pierced one wall,
So you stoop to go on in. The spring,
Five outlets in a wide
Arc (cold star), whence gushes
Crystal water still,
They housed it in a shrine, you see

Here the huge root spread:
A willow hit by lightning, long
Before we came. Before the roof caved in,
Trees all around,

Their graves in the rock, under a green hood
They heard willow speak to water,
And housed the spring, so it could dwell
In itself, as such a place might wish to.
Yes, dwell in itself.
     Yes, them, not us.

Dead Button: China Command Aircrew

Now the dead button does not stick,
Where should we put it? The rock face
We hit, propellers feathering, off the map,
Provided our skeletons, but first
Sorrow, deep, no news, a lacuna cut out

In the air. Twenty-six I was, ships below.
Our bombs away we headed for home.
No home. Told it was under attack, we
Deviated, where to, beneath us brown
Rice-paddies, we supposed, then up

Soaring toward those mountain temples
Ancient painters faintly inked in.
Off the map. Again we deviated, where
Nothing spoke, the radio spat and crackled,
Rock was it, or sea? A bad situation.

So you take hold on the controls and hope;
It is a ghostly moment when the engines quit;
And everywhere there was a whispering,
Which explains the blank looks on our faces.
The first thought, of *mom* and *dad*

Or *little sister*, soon forgot. No whiff
Of pinewood. No warmth of Dairy Queen. We
Feathered another minute, numb, then the impact.
Our different fuses blew all pictures out.
And fifty years it took for an old man

To crawl up close to the ice, with his sack,
Hunting for rare herbs, a Chinaman,
Real old, in a straw hat, raggety pants,
A bit puffed, he cursed between his teeth –
If we'd lived, how fiercely our skeletons

Would have jumped from the wreck, waving,
Taken him into their arms, felt him solid.
As it was, the dead button still stuck.
They dragged us down, there being in us
Money. Then the ceremony of bones. A story,

Heaven sent for commerce between their systems,
Those peevish faces, those bugles, flags,
High beliefs in freedom emptied our air.
So the merchants' fingers hit the buttons,
They counted advantages to be got, pronto.

We'd have liked it otherwise, kindlier,
Tunnels of glaze, Peruvian sigils mounted
On silk, beer, female fur, vaginas.
A ukelele melody fluttering, a blue jay call.
Harvey always wanted to visit Leningrad.

The Glummonging

Ah, Thomas Chatterton, I hear
They cut you short,
Those tittering, merry English,
Their phrasing sold, imagination bought.

Your archaisms, real thing or no –
The *peede chelandri*, *faitour*, *autremete* –
Ne buttoned up in golde your tommy rot,
You laid it at their flat field marshal feet.

Those eighteenth-century smooth gentlemen
Booted your writ away;
Your syntax made a lattice for the tongue,
A *welken* game their tut-tut could not play.

Pundits looking down ignoble noses,
Comfortable in their camphor privy Lent,
Poohpoohed the new life singing in decay,
Smelled in your Carnival only excrement.

You had divined the slithy worst in their
Relaxed iambics, unction, politesse;
Your diction was too crannied for the toffs –
Crystal resistance, not a *clymmynge* mess.

Easily said: imagination, phrasing,
Bought and sold – so what of me?
Unhailie vagabond, am I your abbot,
Riding easy, you *binethe* your tree?

Your aim was high, your elbow only
Swung at an angle too far out:
Still the tubs of grease they trade in
Glummong the rebel shout.

Gentle Reader

In Salieri's Concerto for flute, oboe, and strings
The second movement brings to life a landscape:

Of poplars by a silver river, slender trees
Shimmering in the river, in the air. At noon

The music and the landscape are reciprocal:
Fields, a horseman trots across, and stops,

Soon he is hiding, just an elbow and a hat,
Beneath a tree; his back is propped against it.

The horse, its bridle dangling, crops the grass,
Enjoys the cool, the chirrup of a wren, perhaps.

Oboe, flute, and strings deliver from the air
Just such a picture, like a Claude Lorraine.

Another fifty years – with different trees
The picture will be mistier, Corot.

Greedy for images, gentle reader,
On the web you surf, or on a tattered page

Rescued from a dust heap, what you read –
You need not think its product in your mind

Resembles in the least what's being written here.
Salieri knew the worst but never saw

In 1942 the Lithuanian women,
Their hard-worked hands given so little time

To shield their breasts, cover their genitals,
The looks upon their faces blank,

Stripped to be shot into a pit
Not yet quite filled with other naked corpses,

Nor did he hear the shouts of thugs
Clubbing to death with crowbars people

Rather shocked to find that this was happening
A few doors only from home, for no good reason,

And happening to them, in their marketplace.

Another fifty years, imagine, gentle reader,
And other women, other men . . .

The Swallow Diver

The swallow diver, but of course, when the owl
    Is calling, not Minerva's, late in the day,
And slowly the swallow diver comes to mind

For the owl in a way tells they still exist,
    These oaks, in an ordinary neighbourhood
Yet rooted in earth by systems intricate

As the acorn interior to a grievance –
    Ancient grudge – and the dead are unappeased,
For it is tough, the human fabric, said the owl,

The owl that tells of hurt still to be done,
    Of the damned, of slaves, of the decomposed
Who haunt this tract of earth, at this little

Window asking to be named. Did they belong then
    To nobody, the swallow diver's antics? The moment
When foot lifted, wheel stopped spinning

And there it stood, the Chinese jar, for nobody
    In that moment, furnace cool as yet, before
Twigs took and the fire began to roar,

Then the swallow diver breaks the pool surface,
    Hollows the pool but fits snug in the hollow.
The moment of his descent through water,

How long anticipated? How to judge its emphasis,
    Until his body turns, arching, and spirals
Back to the air, to air in an interval, one only,

The interval between the crematory rages
    Escapes in the spring of the swallow diver,
The board booms and in mid-air he jackknives

To meet in a moment, head-on, the water, so
    To spear it, through, and has arched
His backbone, soaring up, once to whisk his head

And breathe again, as in all likelihood
    An acrobat feels the plummeting trapeze
Bar slot into his palm, and breathes again.

For so it was. The interval is over.
    It was a verb that sounded and was foreign,
Kin to a tongue the sun dries a stone with;

If the swallow diver has altered the water
    Into a sole blue star for a moment,
By name Anemone, no pool remembers it.

A Saint in Japan

Is it shock or boredom or disgust
Appearing in his face? The lips
Are shut, with corners turning down,
But only as if they might turn up
If a duck or blue heron under his gaze
Simply behaved in the mirror of its pond.

Look again: not shock or boredom or disgust,
But sorrow. Horrible
Occasions have not passed him by. Nothing,
Nothing has been lost on him. The tilt
Of his oval head, eyes untypically open
Forage into the thick of things –
What can that tilt, this look, happen to mean?

That with compassion tearing at him a man
Can still be all of a piece? That a joke
Might be told well enough in his presence
And he would chuckle at it.
And that the "peace" would not be "disturbed",
Carnage in the street, a blood slick
In which he might slip, if, serenity itself,
He found his way there.

                          Was he actually
So, or did the artist, here,
To placate a tyrant or to please himself,
Project the head, the folds of a robe,
The fingers joining, thumb tips in touch,
Project this tough nut with human features
To contain in clay the hollow not to be seen?

And for how long had the rebel disappeared,
Huge boles of bamboo sprouted
Where a bewildered old man often sat
Finding not a thing more sensible to do
That fathom crow flight, brainwork of the ant?

That he might not, when all in a flash
The foul and hurt out-there evaporated,
Be quit of fellow-feeling, naked thought,
The breathless saint exhales
Imagination on a mahogany chair
And with beauty ripples his clinging
Terracotta robes – what a wish, not hollow.

Can this codger be taunting all the world
To wiggle free of its pupa, violence?
When the lights go out, still the figure is there.
When frogs call, he is listening still.
Some ceremony he expects, but not such
As might turn the tea sour or the gods off.

That look is the look of a man who knows
He does not know it all, has only choices,
Not answers; and forgot that we might look
At an image of him, look back, having questions.
Yet he knew that a potter with a skill
Might one day hear of him –
Old crosspatch who haunted one or two
Faulty memories and spoke little –
And pound some clay to fit him into,
Lift him up for show: "Look hard now,
Partake of this."

A Square Look in Slant Light

La couleur est une mesure
                    – Claude Royet-Journoud

The colour
a measure

She flies
in pursuit

of objects we
(knowing her)

know next
to nothing of –

*

Which was which?
Human time

techno-
philiac

faster
than ever –

willing yet
seeming bereft

of a will
to be distinct

I might shuck
chimeras off

only to drift twixt
clashing rocks.

*

Maybe blue
is dust, good

wicked.
Appended

icons burn up
senseless

sooner
than you may think –

Holy Vomit!
Such a flux –

*

Such bravura
yet again

nothing settles,
later, elsewhere

in the nick
of time you'll sift

grey from pink,
short from long,

devote yourself
to a dark task,

rise for once
fortunate

to walk on air
as they foretold,

grains in your cup
sedimented.

*

Nomads of old,
luckier far

than us, how come
it felt right,

one pair of feet,
one pony's back

– but milk, Omar –
did it for now

and that blood
is fire, bone

wilderness, towns
powder, you

could not believe.
A variant

bird call, changes
of the light,

temperatures
and waterways

were homing signs:

*

earth not yet new

is earthier,
gunshot or

ocatillo,
that scorpion flower,

the deadlier,
redder,

simply
for being so.

An Open Door

The atmospherical metaphors
    And visions on a mountain top
Never did placate the vague
    Tormentor. Willing to play

Agent of our deeds, in her
    Breasted body bag, or his
Goat with a clatter disappearing
    Into the mist on a scree,

Both, for sure, having needs,
    Stank and were pure,
And they gave rise, they did,
    To a torrent of artifice:

Everlasting debate, balding heads
    Busy with orbs and wars,
Triangles, nutrients, the fashion
    For ceremony and pierced feet,

Columns that strode erect with fans
    And roofbeams to regularize
The maze of space, not to mention
    Time, to each a measure of it,

Still contained the breath
    From a grasshopper's wing
Or a crack regiment. Now arcanely
    The black stray cat slinks in,

And here it is, a silence, again
    Isolable, coated in fluff,
For humility becomes the cat
    Reminding me of them.

Yet artifice only diminishes,
    Language airily displaces,
Any sense of an *It*. Catching
    Like flesh on a thorn,

Truly thought is ripped
    And settles for less than a bison
In rock, a fish in a sliver
    Of limestone, flat;

The hand, its negative imprint
    Lifting all heaven to beckon out
Responsible kin, presses the glory
    Back, and the horror, of *Them*.

Septuagenarian Goethe Musing

Day or night they sweep
A darkness from the sky,

Carrying eyes and thrones,
Our continents and foaming

Vats of liquor, faces
Of people we have fought,

People we have loved. Ancient
Nobles populate our clouds,

Even the spawn of squatting frogs
Helps to condense the drama.

Forget the clouds, murky monsters
Flying to the north tonight:

Was that not a friend came by?
Did not need to be persuaded?

So you ate, so you drank.
When the ginger cat strode in,

Happening on you, just like that,
It gobbled up a chicken skin.

Such a clean and rosy mouth.
What music haunted then your head?

And when they gripped the fork,
How solid your friend's fingers,

When he swallowed wine,
How huge his gullet. How

Nice you were not . . .
Badgered by police, or blown

Skyhigh for nothing by a bomb.
How ungraspingly tonight,

Phantoms of thrones, tonight benign,
They cruise across the sky, our clouds.

2

With a Flute in Provence

Sackbut and viol, the wind and the cords
Lick around this room with a white
Beamed ceiling, skyblue walls;
And this medievally quick

Strangled music, why hear it happily
So, on a sofa? Better from elsewhere,
Better to hear it, ghostly, from the street,
Better to want to be in there, and alone.

Who hears it inside these blue walls
Imagines a cave. Caskets of treasure
Flip their creaking lids, one by one,
Wide open. And the air, the air

Is cool, cool with musk and lavender.
A cave, how lit? Do the golden tissues,
Ruby-crusted diadems and whatnot,
Flood with a glow that secret place?

God knows, it was a sublimate, the music.
Terror, greed, butchery, and plague
At every turn – composers knew
How shit-kickers clung to the mud in those days.

But how the room justifies sorcery, explain that.
Throw the shutters open: on the paving
Down below, snails have made with slime
Silver tracks, for early sun to swallow.

Go figure. Now a housewife takes to song,
Crawl back along the street, listen,
Listen for it. Peer into the young cupped
Palms and into old ones, cratered, these

That have no home to hurry to, and nothing,
Nothing to hold: hear it dwindle there.
Or else with a flute
Whose keys a lightning touch triggers

Tell of the begging on every level,
For food, for work, for a piece
Of the beauty, a lick of the calm,
For a nip, no more, of the holy one.

Between Two Owl Hoots

A foot or two
    Yet far away
The mouth wide open
    And a thousand
Glittering needle teeth
    The mouth – no lips –
Bared fangs more like
    Or is it scooped

Out of the mountain
    A cavern crammed
With shining dancers
    Transfixed as if
All motion slipped
    Between two owl hoots
Off their swarming
    Selfless flesh

– But do not blink
When palaeophobias
    Froth up again
Or stay too long
    Or smiling soon submit
Again to the norm
    Stand on the rim
An instant outside in

That was a pine
That was your piddle
   A flashlight moon
Cleaving the scope
   Of lonely branches
Made them glitter
   Stand on the rim
Vertical vertical

The mother of worries
   This was her jawbone
The uncle of actions
   This was his snout
Go undeceived
   By owl or raven
The painted show
   The bust of Pallas

But touch the tree
   In time the roots
With stars conspiring
   Clasp and lift you
One hoot for death
   So they did say
Two for the stories
   You can question

The Red Restaurant

Beautiful not, but positively
One neat woman – her slant eyes
    Remind him of someone, back home:
The spatulate nose, retroussé, but long,
Hair drawn back in a blonde wave,
    Her nape in its bush. Now she tilts her head,
Downcast for a second sip, for emphasis
Spreads her fingers, but brightening; even
    The whosit she smiles for, might he be Tim?

And what kind of poem is this? Back home,
Sooner or later, sighting again the original,
    He'll wonder who she reminds him of.
What kind of a poem, if it's her he finds
Reminding him of a woman to be counted on
    In another place, a heartthrob
He cannot identify, let alone the haunting
Red restaurant she chose
    Twice to appear in?

Karin's Parakeet

No face to speak of, eyes
Inconspicuous, the beak vestigial
But a glossy torso, streamlined,
And tail feathers erigible, echoing
A razor shell. Let him hop,

She said, and from her finger to mine
The parakeet (each wingtip twice
Trimmed with a pelmet of driven snow)
Did hop, only to ratchet crabwise,
Yet elastically, up and up,

As if drawn by some force or friction,
Past the elbow to my cotton shoulder
And perched, out of sight, looking back,
Out of mind, into whatever it saw
Back of my back, so light this bird,

Having scaled my arm as a reptile might,
Could be forgotten. They had placed
Before me a glass of wine and a square meal.
The parakeet, no cat, wanted no part of it,
But I made a hopeful bird sound,

Letting my tongue's tip click liquidly
Against the palate, and then to the fore
That white, weightless bird swivelled.
So for a time we talked, the clicks
Alternating with tail flip and whistle.

It was not long before the parakeet
Discovered I had nothing at all to say . . .

Then he was picking at my ear, the ridges
And craters, arroyos of rose and tone,
For all I knew; significant hairs
Or particles of dried sweat drew the bird
As facts of life, to be enjoyed, for now,

Now he really got going into it
Ardent as an archaeologist who, having sighted
Chips of flint near sundown shining
On top of earth fresh turned by the plough,
Will map their densities, keys to culture.

But if ever I backed off, he'd whistle,
Only to be consoled by another triple click
Which drew him out of a fugitive chagrin
And on again, to deepen his inspection:
My ear, I felt him (breath inaudible) shyly

Circle it, deep inside, something
He did not need to know spelled
Dabu kadar kalehra, though he chose
Not to peck at it. Any moment,
I was thinking, he will penetrate – what then?

He did not. My clicks kept him
Comfortable with me. We had an African
Relationship. He understood, beyond a doubt,
How stealthily I'd focus my binoculars
Whenever a crow or kestrel

Alights on the tip of the telephone pole
Between my door and sky to the south-east.
Something in his body was one with that.
But what that is, a plenum
Of air which changes the hollow

Dome into a bond complecting,
Articulate, our actual
And imaginary gestures, only the parakeet
Might then have known,
In its diminutive and vulnerable song fluff

Known a vast
Congenial aurora – the ear
Of a creation we so insistently desire
Might catch whatever
It is we were meaning to say.

Feuilleton 3: Alchemy of the Word

Manuel Bey, born about 1935, in Istanbul,
Sephardic Turk, fluent in Portuguese,
Spanish, Italian, competent in French,
Bears the head and features of Gustave Flaubert.

And Flaubert, that November, on his Oriental Journey,
"Limbic" Flaubert, who fancied women small,
Dark, and fiery, did he plunge into
Une existence gorge-de-pigeon, having dined
In Pera with the French Ambassador?

Manuel Bey (his line is global business)
Claims there is nothing he can't buy and sell.
Robust, athletic, shirt of denim, blue jeans,
Underneath the Cappadocian stars
Philosophizing with a metallurgist,
Never at a loss for words.

Nietzsche's Hands

Celebrated, the moustache,
And near enough ignored
His "beautiful hands".

Capable on a keyboard, improvised
A polonaise, his own artistic
Compositions "dull and decent".

He could see, some, but much swam, out there:
Knives and forks, print, street signs.
Then, his mind made up, he laid about,

Sank immense nets into the cultural acid.
When he winched them back in, on fingertips,
They rippled with rainbows – herring and sprat

He could fling, raw, in the teeth
Of the *Bürgertum*, God rot it. Ah, no God:
So to invoke the impact of quanta on quanta

And extirpate for keeps the German cabbage,
His fingers, subject to whim, and rounded
Like objects in a metaphor, made good the feeble

Peering eyes. Each tip housed a labyrinth,
Circling in or out, from ivories an octopod
Pressed the torrent of a tune. From Cretan pots

Their gestures, snaking out, apprehended,
Turn on turn, a tumbril in the stars.
Those fingers must have held, no less, the comb

To bush his hairy icon out, to primp.
On long mountain walks they jotted Gothic
Letters on a page, deleted angrily

Brainwaves, on a page one trouser leg
Segregated from his knee. What a joy,
At long last, to know the knower not deceived

But disobedient, at his word. Underneath
The creams of language here's a tongue can taste
A universe, cyclopic, but propulsive, alien

To a species blocked by self-torment,
To shopping, authority – all the cockahoop
Engines of flesh not fuelled by despair.

When Nietzsche, squinting, trimmed his fingernails,
Did he care for suchlike slighter things?
To a turning pot a potter's fingers do not cling.

Is there no Name for what we are Losing?

Finally we found it: a square of dust.
Ancient walls festooned with moss and flowers;
Not far the hoot, again, of a little owl,
Drop by drop in water. And laundry hung
High on the walls, bedsheets, shirts, pantaloons
Danced in sunlight, taking the good air in,
While a boy on a bicycle rode around
And small shops invited our attention.

Yet this, after all, was not the place.
You know its touch: a cold oblivion.
How does a real thing come to haunt a picture?
Distance is not contracted on a road map,
Monsters on impulse crave to be included.
Postcards, anyway, gave the place a name
Not the one stuck in our craw that morning.

They told us: Up the hill your other place,
See? Turn south, but why? Nothing there.
Still, if you wish it. So uphill we went,
Found the dirt road and cruised along it;
Treeless fields, weeping meadowlarks flew past
And the day's journey advanced longer and longer.

Then we saw it: west, the lake, the twin hills,
Vaulted, steep as if constructed. One
With a house on top, bald as an egg the other.
Shorn hills and the lake stagnant, dwellings next,
Of pink stone, or darker, coral, derelict,
But several held up as best they could,
And the track snaked up among the cottages,
Broken cobbles, difficult now to walk on.

And rising south a slope came into sight,
The slope we had so long been drawn to,
Conical mountain peak beyond it, ways off.
It levelled out and over that plateau,
Featureless in a vast and glowing atmosphere,
Thousands of heaped stones absorbed the twilight.

Their presence hit us first, a shock,
Then all at once our own, striking downward,
Through lung and heart, as heron strikes a fish:
Our own Byzantine barracks, shook to the ground
By centuries or earthquake. – Soon tinkling through
Came a straggle of sheep, headed for home.
Dogs. Children. Touching his knitted cap
An old man on a donkey nodded his selam,
For things had gone wrong, plenty, in his lifetime.

Armies from the south, scattered to roost.
Armies from the east shrank back to Diyarbakır.
Now not so sinister, marked on one map in ten,
The citadel, untrumpeted, the squalid lake:
Vigilant hilltops haven't a thing to do;
Even the ablutions you would not understand.

But can it be kept, the secret of a place?
Diggers will be hired, analysts of earth,
Scholars to sift and measure, lift up skulls,
Masons to dress archways afresh and set them
Foursquare, historic and substantial.
Will a stone shatter, crying out for sheep?
No children sprout from crevices of dew?
Busloads of people soon will be dragooned
Around the bakery, through the necropolis,
And afterward settle, yawning, in the tea house.

Strange, those we thought we had forever killed,
When they come, it will not be to kill us.
They will confer, point, be interested.
What if one, alone, go so deep into the marvel
He comes back flighted, whole, the more for love?
No. Soon guides will shout in a host of tongues
Invertible facts, figures that strike no chord –

Just who are they, those people? Surely not
Of other stuff than torturers they hatch.
Yet they will pose to be photographed,
All smiles, among the artfully
Reconstituted quarters of our men, and scoff.

Rodrigo, His Adagio

In a freezing attic,
No room to swing a cat,
Blind Rodrigo his adagio writes.
Blind, he explores the ivory
Piano keyboard and conceives,
Note by note,
In braille a counterpoint.

On the far side of town a hospital,
And sick to death in it his wife:
Horrific grief in his gut, and now
Composing itself in his adagio
A music, think of that.

His frozen fingers travel on the keys,
Note by note their thrusts compose,
Lowly and magical,
A music mapped across the storm
In his amygdala, think of that.

Is it for her, the guitar, to bring her back,
Solo, a plaint, soft notes that surge
Across the scope of hearing you
Now hold out to it; no, it is
For them, the gods, to them

He is showing visions of a hearse
Never seen, though some such
Rushing through dark air and the strain
Of springs that wheels depend on –
He was balancing it between

Eardrum and fingertip:
The flashing rush, the opal glide
Of a certain cadence.

Note by note he shields
From them her breath,
Guarding from them, in their own creole,
The hollows of her body.

Altogether yes, frozen fingertips
Tap out on keys most probably
Out of tune the secret
Parts of those placed instruments,
To shroud the tender notes of one guitar.

Finally in the middle air
He leaves just two or three, to float,
Hesitating,
In hope they may be pleased, and relent,
Those gods, whoever might be there,
And bring her through, home.

Gelibolu

for Marius and Bobbie Kociejowski

I

For the seven minutes it will take, at most,
To slant these figures over their borderlines,
Surprise yourself: Be the lanky waiter
Waving his tray in Çanakkale.
                                        Along the Promenade
People dawdle, arm in arm. He feels a cooling,
Feels in the air a cooling, and he knows –
A multitude of Greeks, Armenians, and Jews,
How they felt it ninety years ago.

II

Soon after eight, at last the sun hangs low.
Somebody signs to him: collapse the parasols.
Under each canopy he takes a stand, reaches up
And puts a thumb against the latch.
A cascade of soft materials is whispering
All around him. Afro song
                            Stopped in its track, he flexes
To the jangle of an oud,
                            Squeal from a clarinet . . .

III

Who knows how it happened in those old days?
Will the lady have taken everything off?
                              A snap, a shrug,
In a torrent of frills and folds
You catch your breath, she catches hers . . .
                              Nevertheless

IV

With octopus arms he plucks the iron stalk
Of each dismantled flower from a socket; slashed
White on red, or red on white, the shrivelled calyx
Blooms again as a barber's pole,
Or hardens as a peppermint stick.
Now he clasps them, one by one, lopes
Sighing across the broken paving stones,
And has dropped his trophies in the shadows, flat.

V

Nonchalant now he stands and sweats,
                              Sinister hero,
Hearing the gulls cry, a little dazed
                              By so much clarity.
The last moment, sweetest when it comes –
Over the thud of ferryboat engines, a whiff
Of grilling fish delights his nose,
                              And here she rides,
The schoolgirl, on her bicycle. She brings
For him her smile. And from one handlebar
She has unhooked her twitching fish bag.

VI

I wonder: do I turn my gaze to the hills?
Does he acknowledge those huge burned hills?
The soldiers flit there, Anzac and Turk;
Ghost mouths agape, asking for water, water,
They bumble toward the doorway by starlight.
I have heard tell old villagers oblige them.

VII

Can I lift, now the waiter downs his tray,
A last glance, even, to the hills?
                              Convex craters,
Ivory on dusk, the honeycombed efficiencies for him
Have no possible interest, constructed there
Some distance from the graves,
A more or less decent distance from the graves.

Tin Flag and Magpie

A tin flag and a magpie face
Each other over roofs I know;
A stiff tin flag turns in the wind,
A magpie perches close behind.
The world is an entangled place
Whichever way the wind may blow.

The stiff tin flag is black, the bird
Likewise, but port and starboard wings,
Paunch no less, the snows ignite:
Analogy intercepts all things
That pour their forms through curves of light,
So ghostly harmonies can be heard.

The flag a wing, the magpie's voice
Creaks, as if it were hoisted high
On a mast atop an old clocktower;
By chance a chord was struck, but our
Flagbird, on an urge to fly,
Quit the picture then by choice.

Those things go, disentangled, free,
Whichever way the wind had blown;
Shattering schemes of you or me
A flag revolves, a bird has flown –
Our objects, humble, they aspire;
Learn we our ashes by their fire.

[*Malaucène, Vaucluse*]

48

Feuilleton 5: The Buskers

Four buskers almost balkanized, tonight,
August 4th, the Place de la Contrescarpe.

Every one of them in wind and limb complete,
The accordionist all but a hunchback –

After the first melodious flourishes were done,
The clarinet began to take his instrument apart,

Blowing shorter tunes, to show the way it worked;
But on a keyboard hanging from his neck

The carpenter pianist banged out routine chords
And the violin a beanpole man was fingering

Sliced through the edges of catalpa leaves
With long shrieks, rat trills, and all in fun.

Cars now orbiting the quadrangle of trees
Turned into tubes filled with human meat,

Noses took the scent of carnage from their lager
(Even so, the buzz of talk, no way to stop it)

And cherry red the sanitation mobilette,
Cherry red the track suit of its rider,

The sliced leaves, iron chains that link
Old mooring posts around the beds of flowers,

Fogged the eye with fright, and meaning trouble
Identical white camper caravans

Rolled into view, the one behind the other,
For thugs to jump from, us to be flung into.

Rohmahniyah! he shouts, shaking his money pot,
The clarinettist, *Ceausescu, fini!* Whereupon,

Classic features, stepping light and fresh
From reeds that told secrets of a beauty parlour,

A nice Missouri girl, in green, with pearls
To plug each earlobe, pushed her wicker chair aside;

Showing a dainty midriff, on steady legs
She strolled across the street, as if to depollute

With every breath, every stride, the air
Our music for a moment had inhabited.

Then the white, lost caravans came back again,
Carnation milk inside, stringbags of potatoes,

Family snug inside, in each a Belgian grandpa,
Peering every which way, at the wheel.

Loom is Being Granular

This room, too thin, nothing hot in it,
A thousand books, carpets nomad women wove

And daybreak when, splendid on a piece of ham,
Enormous light diagonally slices in –

Still I make my exit, eyesight eases up
And down the book spines, nose takes comfort,

Off I careen, down the steps, a tumult
For scattering cats, how graceful, them,

Though it happens I am long gone to Berlin,
Haunting whose saloons, destination Belgrade,

Pretend dead, play possum beneath bullets
If only I could burrow through the flagstones

For Istanbul is next and means choosing
Free speech in a certain torture chamber,

Only in Antioch, more precisely Daphne,
Am I released, for dumping in the sea

Still at the foot of my steps, still here,
Not along the continuum, O no, the elastic

Broke, groove split, creamy voice knocked it off,
And reconsider the room and me, liar, in it

And the sea crashing through it, thoughts
Loom, purple, and tastes fade into cheese,

Sensation as on a quivering ship of wood
When it turns about, into the wave's whack,

And if it crests, hot slit, matters not one bit
To the moon. So my orbit, back up and home,

Draws out threads and rams them forward in,
The while, archaic, cloud cools my head:

What's to do out there, this music lacking?
I marvel then that shipwrights, long ago,

Fitted their pine planks and braced them
With mortice orthogonal and tenon, tight;

As masons might pitch a temple roof
Foursquare on tenuous illusions of oval,

Dancers danced to it, in a ring their muscle
Wove to contain, 'confusedly regular,

The moving maze' or to transform the season
Their twin rows with a shriek of flutes meet

Spinning, in, out, for their pomegranate housed
A thousand pips, soon apart, soon again together.

3

The Redbird Hexagon

1

REDBIRD

It waylaid my eye
On the loose,
As it obscurely scaled
The staff of a Venetian blind.

Now behind the open slats,
Beyond the windowpane,
Busy among the cedar forks
A figure was distinct:

Beyond the books, their spines,
Outside, and south,
A throat, a thorax. –
To judge

By the silhouette,
It should be red. It could be.
Then how is presence felt?
Can time undo deformity?

Southern twilight now descending,
Dull cedar green devoured
The colour hot – and solo
A profile agitated

The retina. A saucy crest,
A tail that flipped,
Perfect balance
Lost in a wink, in a wink recovered.

No fanfare whatsoever,
Volume, until dauntless
Off your twig
You quit the signature:

Then, songbird, I assumed
Your absolute disguise,
As from his eyes
A horned toad spits red liquor.

OF THE NAUTILUS

Late, into the night,
Touch the nautilus, unwinding,
Winding. Its mathematical,
Its oceanic equations, which
Aspect is then
Your finger to rest on?

                    Curving,
The shell gets warmer
In your palm, vacant sleeper;
Along with it you meant to have
Some kind of dream,

Secret at the far
End of the tunnel: but another
Day broke. So was the dream
The void itself of all those
Images that return, return

To be shot, forgotten
At the first whistle
Of a little wren?

              Otherwise, first thing,
In a taste of bergamot, or else
Later, on the treadmill, dare you
Say, during an interval,
Through the smoke of a cigarette,
Out of nowhere comes back the dream,
Full flush, already disappearing:
. . . and words drove them, these –

"Sacred rage", a multitude of peoples:
On horseback; building forts; adrift;
Some to throng the air, where
Faint harp chords sounded very deep;
Some few who smile and huddle
In a dry cave, the boy carving the flute –

Borders thrust up gradually to subdivide
The fluid. So thickly
Crystallizing steel and glass cones
Circle the cubic hollows, the explosives,
Anaxagoras.

        Any moment now,
And real sacred rage, for the multitudes
Invert, convex, driven by new words
Headmen enact afresh ancient evils,
Calamitous compulsions.

        Whatever they were aiming at
Extinguished every flicker of it.
A token incised in a tablet of clay,
A hovel, storage for a minotaur,
A myth of maybe, infinite, consoling,
Gratified one savage heart, another not.

Fast as they built, slow as they drifted,
There is a power streams to lift up back
To the light their luminous faces.
        A fear of it
Dimmed their faces. To touch them only,

Recognize, love a lunar distance
In the parabola of a cheekbone,
Almost home – of that light in feeling
Has a history been told yet?

                    Vomit and blood
Spangle the traces of these persecutors
Who are hooded;
Having no passion for that,
Hoppity in their traces, hoppity whistles
The little wren.

3

PRIMA MATERIA

In this knothole I can hear them clearest.
I prop my head in my hands and listen.
These are human voices you might wish to hear.
Voices in the night from a balcony across the way.
Voices in the night have brushed other sounds aside.

*

From this knothole you can peer through the juniper.
Peer over the narrow potholed street.
Peer through the branches of ornamental pomegranate.
Then you pick out the distant fairy lights.

*

What they say on the balcony cannot be understood.
What I like is hearing voices only in the Spring night.
Voice, in the invisible hand a complicated plaything.

*

Sudden gusts of laughter breach the murmur.
Under gunfire they will remember this conversation.

*

Go by all means where none has gone before.
Still the silence around the voices concedes no evil.
Old as the hills they make not a noise but a sound.
No need to hold onto it, let the voices go.

*

Listen, listen, and let the voices go.
A bit of a mystery, this.
The rim of a mystery spinning very fast.
Any least touch burns away your hand.

TRIPLE CODA

Through the glass flesh shone essential light,
    And that was the Always Other, who has come
        To winch our cracked old pitchers up
Out of a clogged well. What if they shine again?

A thought, gentle Zeno, so fragile. Give me time
    To think it when the bullet stands half its way
        To the back of my skull, or still distant
It sizzles from the infinite pinpoint.

*

This widow on a mountain may not enter Macedonia.
Her child died of hypothermia in the night.
Holding the child she has cried her heart out.

The dew shaken from a tree by the wind
Still looks for kindness from the dust.

*

    We have buried
The treasure under our tackle:
      Resplendence;
And community we have ranked
      In the order of things
Far behind commodity; to everything superior,
      Ravenous ego.

There is a surge
      Crusted by existence,
The crust thickening

The surge is dispersed.
On the march
    In progressive reverse
Who'll dance for the dance, the dancer,
    For the flavour of it?

With stuff and more stuff
    Blindfolded,
How should the limpid souls look on
    And indicate what is what,
The great souls, among asphodel?

        Over the heads of crooks,
Scorpions attired in tinsel,
        A sack splits, the downpour
Is fetid, delirium.

        So climbing, still a tremor,
Stair on stair, to the throne,

The surge that shook the Spring night murmured,
To make it sing, clear, six notes, the redbird.

[Note: Lines 4-5 in the second coda come from Ts'ui's letter
to Chang in "The Story of Ts'ui Ying-Ying" by Yüan Chen
(AD 788–831). See Arthur Waley, *More Translations from the
Chinese*. New York, Alfred A. Knopf, 1937, p.114.]

4

To the Ghost of my Grandmother, Anne Shepherd

My garden too, I cultivated it –
Some of the bulbs were not molested
By these raccoons, these armadillos; others
Were gnawed by a spectre, aching love.
It was a garden of artemisias,
Reliefs, anxieties, moss from Kolyma.

A fringe garden, *locus amoenus*, a park,
A point of light, a pinpoint on a globe,
The globe of English that encompassed it;
Large, ancient, fathomless, in my time
That globe pupped for Caesar
A pingpong ball, for Cassius a shuttlecock.

My schoolgirl garden – I wanted
To shelter you, not in a crypt but openly
To prove your bright whirling in the teeth
Of atrophy: in nameless pods new plagues
Beamed down to earth by avarice
Torture the poor, set fire to the forest.

I was putting around my schoolgirl
A picket fence; good sound for whitewash,
Twisting jokes and ironies to wire
Any solemn aha not worth a cuss.
A wobbly fence; yet halfways it admitted
Colour and scent into the bells of hyacinth.

What if I'd had the buried stream
Rushing clear, entire, articulate
Through my bones? I had a trickle only,
And diverted it. Other languages,
In them a purity might exist.
A foreigner I felt them to be pure.

Wrong. Still, if one unbeaten track
Shone with mutant myth, it held a promise,
Half holy to the foreigner, at least
Seeming so, because his mother, on the floor,
Was being poked in every orifice at random,
By each gross faction claimed, by all abused.

O schoolgirl garden, I do not forsake you.
I'm here. See me flourish my trowel,
Shoulder my sack of propitious horse dung.
Yet I do wish I'd felt, filling imagination,
The sympathetic breath that still compounds,
Ins and outs, the thin red line of English.

Generosity, flexion, tautness, lift –
Call it *give* – how sunlight
Scuds across our hills, how it spawns the talk
Even in Cornish villages. How blue
And silver flashes turn our spires, spokes
Of an old cartwheel grinding through wine bars.

The bittern booming from his rushes . . .

And a twitter of linnets riding the breeze.
Almost Ovid. No. I echo oblivion,
Thinking. A migrant on the loose
Cares for his country still, but his tongue –
That he would rather eat than claim
A sentimental home he chose to quit.

Grandmother, I have not gone far enough.
Anne Shepherd, milkmaid, when you sang
Ditties to the cows, how cold was it?

How did you keep them soft, your fingertips?
Your children, how did they come to music
If not through your gift? You went in, I out.

Be with me now. Open the English book.

Antiquity with Epithets

etiam recente terrae sola sanguine maculans
niveis citata cepit manibus leve tympanum
— Catullus LXIII

Evening stroll along the wharf,
Fishing boats, Halo, Sunbeam:
Sacred to Cybele, gouged in the rock
A vacant shrine, prows angled at it
Risk a smile.

Near sundown
A steely blue invades the harbour,
And on a box, for sale, trinkets glitter.
Little rabbits huddle on the box;
Round their throats the whiskered
Trinket man, all thumb and finger,
Hooked ribbons — blood and silky
Red, to trap the eye;

hot red
To slit the bag of memory open:
For instance, Agamemnon;
Also splashed against her bathroom tiles
Unhappy Mrs Herington.
Sometimes you only see
Oyster people walking past. Sometimes,
Pouring out of every head,
A red webbing very like a parachute.

What's in a man to choose what he remembers?
One voice only tells him:
                    Don't forget the rabbits –
They huddle on the box, the fingers of
The trinket man force down their heads: a slip
Of paper that they bite will tell your fortune.

Those rabbits, how they sniffed the fishy air
And held it in
Their pussywillow bodies – not for long.

[*Eski Foça*, 1995]

Tussock Moth

However stiff, having eaten
Of several trees,
The solo cadaver,
Nobody comes to touch it. Joy
Has taken the night off. The object, even so,

What now, a coupling occurs,
Here, a moth, to be identified, by name,
Waits for it. The feelers erectile,
Forelegs cradle an ellipse. Those wings

Are folded copper. Stir as it may,
When you stroke it,
Soft Sphinx in a tobacco sheath,
We face it,
A death, I mean, and hear the beams
Of a hollow ship –

Friction of woof against
My warp and the whole creaking fabric
Woven through starlit
Shores I do not forget, if only
Echo, my nymph, in the deep flow
Parades her limbs – begin to break apart.

So there, in anger or else disgust,
One of us has to stand up and smartly
Flit into the kitchen, do the dishes.

A palace in your body, bright moth,
Contracts. The candelabra go dim,
Yawning patrons
Quit you, downstairs the people
Wash their hands, brush their outfits,
And descend on the village to dance.

Adagio in the Shipyard

Traits there are,
Traits you happen to follow, in earth
Ravines cloven by the ploughshare,
Wet, and wedged in the earth
Pressure-flaked a flint tool,
A skin scraper.

A smell of coal, how it curdled
In that back yard the air around you.
And Hector Llewellyn, scrum half,
Plucked out and flung the ball, his body
Flew full-stretch and still, as he did so,
Is suspended in the middle air.

The traces, which way do they go
Back or on? Up, too. Never quite
Levitating, the dancers. Not knowing why,
You took to the darkening theatre. Distant
Arms, all at once they cleft the air
And with light feet that made no sound
How come their flesh folds into a rose?

Around the disc of bronze, magic letters:
Rare, the sestertius of Pertinax,
Rarer the silver horses galloping right
And Syracusan Arethusa, her
Streaming hair and ghost of a dimple.

None of this had to lead anywhere. Each
Instant of uplift
Secretes (does it?) a church bell. Recalled
Or prospective time, incised in it
Every trace of there and then, here and now

Might have pronounced the note,
Conspired the sign from another world.

But no melody selects itself.
Even your dead do not lie still.
Everything sickens the heart,
For it has chosen not to stop beating;
Back and forth its bellnotes
Swing, take their toll, so modulate,
But the swirl of the world, its offing,
They do map it.

A haze constellates, the new ships
Hoist orange sails, happening to loom
Through: sharper prows, lighter poops, masts,
Look, they balance broadening day,
Dancers need no decks,
Their arms reach out, embrace, as if
It were nothing, the wind.

Recovering Dream

A feathery tip of something traced from under
The prospect, not the action, of a dream
A feathery sensation; a contour, but relieved
Of any object, grief, or ghoul,
Sprang from a source in me apart from the me
It hardly meant to be remembered by:
A windgust rumples for a wink, like that,
A furlong of the sea.

Asleep again I open an old folio:
On buckled sheets of rag paper
A sepia script, the pointy hand of John
Donne moves composing his lost inventions;
Word by word whispered across the page
Squibs to wrench the heart, tumultuous deletions,
Luminous arcades they spanned his globe,
Building up to puzzles, agonies, paradox.

The Dundaries, a light voice fluted soon, in splendour
Outshine the Quandaries; they echo
Stories of strolls in a free city,
Forty-eight fountains, holy sounds, inhabited
Houses in the air, their gardens, all
Of a spiral substance, unpoisoned,
And not satisfactorily explained so far.

Feuilleton 4: A Goldsmith in Cappadocia

That chiselled knob of stone a goldsmith showed me,
I turned it in my fingers – Aphrodite.

Hairdo ruined, chin chipped, nose all but gone:
I told him – *Aphrodit*, look, her expression.

Across afterthoughts I hear him wheeze:
Lonesome infidel, *galiba* he sees

Aphrodit in everything? Suchlike stones
Turn up among clay birds, tiny cows in bronze,

Time and again, when we dig our orchards.
Not so special. Twenty-thirty dollars –

Turned away from the wedding feast . . .
Lips opening to speak to me . . .

Little Red Matchbox

A grey X and a yellow X on a red ground.
A black frame, funeral envelope. Each X
A waiter with a tray on his fingertips.

Oblong on the grey speckled shingles,
Grey shingles of a shining bar counter,
The little red matchbox spilled a green.

A powdery green spilt from the matchbox,
A green – the wings of that enormous moth
Which clung all night to the insect screen,

Green of the emerald moth, like its name,
Mitigated night, black, a throbbing cave,
Insects enough alive in it to melt rock

Gave out their uninterruptible scream.
How come now this green got to be there,
Spilt from the little red matchbox?

Look around. The strings go out from eyes
And trap a silver cocktail shaker, settle
On a red bead in the glass ellipse, your wine.

Or tighten: glimpse the pink profile,
Leaning on her elbow, her legal man
Stiff in a suit, the vanilla sheath

A supple torso, Jessica, pouring gin.
No green, no moth. The matchbox only,
Oblong on the shingle, definitely redder.

Enoptic colours happen. One glance
And all the hues of heaven bounce off
Their complementaries into impish objects

Seen and waiting, waiting to be seen.
Then they perform, concave has swallowed
Convex, yes no, catastrophe elation, starlight

Abysmal time. So now, how to capture
Again that active, uninvited aura,
Green? Let the strings go loose,

Vaguely wandering. A silver cocktail shaker,
A stiff suit, still, a warren of a hairdo –
Not them. See, the strings can swing, softly

Focus revels, later back to the matchbox,
And there the wild intruder is, no question:
The mouse a moment on the threshold, green.

This, exquisite. And you don't notice,
A moon of many watts, hanging steady,
Bathes in the liquors, burns at your elbow,

But the place, this envelope, illuminated,
Rushes on, not knowing any numbers, yet
Multiplying in a flash the shape a tree, say,

Consolidates by pushing through slow centuries:
The space is branching out, blown back or on,
Not knowing which, it fills and spreads

Itself in heads, unforeseen environments,
Hands, little, big, throats drier for the liquid
Speed the place contains turns into spray

As on or back it hurtles. This is what
Not you should see, because, because you ride,
Giving no offence, a lion, ferocious:

This is what spilled from the exploding
Envelope, you and your fugitive smudge
Of green are riding bareback on a dragon.

Party Night at the Yellow Rose

Oftentimes old snouted ladies swarm
To talk their hearts out at the bar;
And their hog men, with skins of whiskey,
Huddle among them, then cut loose
To shoot the breeze about the law.

So they trumpet, so they snort. Vociferous,
They plant on vanishing horizons
All the orange dust their throats
Harbour as paradise, consume as beer.
Flesh squeals under the knife,
Still grunting out the football scores.

Then on their breath you catch a trace
Of something else; and sparse grass tufts
Whisper to contended ground
Grandpa and grandma carpentered a porch upon;
A pang of hunger hits, a whiff of cordite.

Coyotes howl in the pig voice. Apollo
Incinerated all the corn; pier and beam,
To cool the nether air, took in the poison
Fangs of the copperhead. Projectiles
Momentarily suspended in the bar,

Those old buckaroos and ladies hoot
Aromas of a shrivelling religion
Into their food; potted by a child a marigold,
A Mexican shot dead, wounds of their own
By some dimly recalled, load their table too.

An Idle Day in the Dardanelles

1

Flame, there it is, far off
             on the enamel
back of the ocean – sprouting

azalea, a little yacht emits
a volute folded in its flame –

a snowy scoop
or pocket for the wind, waiting for it,
azalea
            who said "on the glistening . . . "?
toil of the sea, hard, lustrous

8 a.m.

2

a powdery dark
            mass bore now down on it

and down on it bore a dark
possible Leviathan

3

Still no wind, the scoop
    ineffectual, points north
       of Lesbos

ah, only a tanker and hm, the spires
            (Marcel in his pony wagon –)
which do not change position
however you may move, connecting, dis-
connecting them:

so
(*loquitur Demokritos*)
     "shape, position, configuration"

            a powdery tanker
still bore down on it.

4

azalea infolded delicate flame
    so snowy white,
a fabric of Byssos being airily thrown
       around a naked woman

but stuck –
    a position, under the

whatever? a position, as if
       in this blue colossal
heat, this
      asthma of an early morning . . .

5

Tenuous the sight lines fix
   variable objects all askew
not wrong, but now heave, so hot it is

         your clutter of bones
half a mile, the shift of a lifetime
   and so have split what looked

coagulant or set to crash – a
   bursting pomegranate fills
with shot the pale
     stiffening village children,

spherical
   geometry of a yacht hull

6

and a day is said to have a middle
     nothing, but a dip
was that a pontoon? was this a dock?

Slide down the iron rungs into the icy
liquid salt, try

         striking south.   Void
"nothing is more real than nothing"

still it was something
        cool, salt, molecular
surround, sheathing live flesh,
surrounding
     a blind spot
        a funk hole

and remember under green oaks a table spread
lampions on the patio illuminating it

purple aubergine, emerald of cucumber
and several reds, tomato, then peppers

sliced in figures of eight, when from on high
a single acorn plopped into my lion's milk

whereupon a black dragonfly spiralled out
and whipped across gunpowder dusk

first one but soon in a frenzy zigzag
splitting the dark air with wings another hovered

and more and more, a hood of dragonflies
capping the oaks, all acorn life let loose

a host of holes and wings and pressures, random
joy held the swarm in place till a south wind,

as the thud of guns, it was Gallipoli
and the crash of armour where they fell at Troy

blew cool that crystal hood of dragonflies
north, we looked again at aubergines

crisp sprats had snowed upon our plates
while Güney sang the song for acorns and the moon.

8

Poem –

Cultivate your secret
or else
when it leaks out
it will be ugly

Placate what is in store,
the pristine, the mayhem, unhatched,
or it will destroy you.
                    No good ever came
of grovelling to ghosts.
                    Answer them kindly.

With feeling clarify

                    latency.

[Note: 'An Idle Day in the Dardanelles' is dedicated to the memory of the "wonderful Snail People". Their myth is recounted in Frank Hamilton Cushing's *Zuni Fetishes* (Flagstaff, 1966), e.g., "Then the earth and winds were filled with rumbling from the feet of the departed animals, and the Snail People saw that their game was escaping, hence the world was filled with the wars of the Kâ'kâ, the Snail People, and the children of men."]

Separate Incidents

Cloud cover breaking up

How, when the music moves so fast
Can that composer's
Hand

Have, with inkblots flying,
Imbricated the notes right
And scratched out none

So slow

While my piano will not
Mark the page
For on their way to the milk bowl
The cat paws left no evidence

Palpable on the carpet

And fur, wet instrument, wrapped
Such expansive appetite, I listen,
I do listen

Amazed that it should glitter, in the sky,
Desire, but sooner or later
Come to myself.

Feuilleton 6: A Sculptor out of Britain

1

There is a green hill far away
Without the wall of Blanco, but, exactly,
Blanco, Texas, has no wall, the hill,
Besides, is not so green, caliche breeds
An archipelago of grey tufts, mid which
(And whistling flowers, bits of rock)
There stands a pole and round it slung,
Warped in a furnace, wrenched, archaic,
Writhes the scrap cadaver of a man.

He who walks upon that hill
About it and about must go:
Oftentimes against the flow,
Like that truth seeker in the verse of Donne.
So Philip John Evett, at seventy-four,
Selects from a rack of them one walking stick,
Then steadily up and round about
His knoll a daily stroll he takes.

2

You look into his sculptures later
From underneath, head-on, at eye-level,
And think the wood, every inch, belongs
To the tree he looked up into, or from its core

Outward. Sound wood he can smell right
And work on, slice, round out, make to tower,
Do a laminated loop, or horned
Cascades conduct your peepers simply
Through a circuit as it flies.

Was it Sunderlands or Ansons, neither,
But Hampdens, in them he flew,
An air gunner, penned
In an egg partly expelled,
There in a pendent bubble Philip squatted,
Thumbs on the triggers, just in case.

He'll say the advantage was that bandits
Rarely hit Coastal Command patrols.
Yet the gun turret under the fuselage
Cramped a man. That landmark on his hill –
It is a monument, believe it, to the full
Stretch of compassion reaching into pain.

3

He had been a boy, ignorant then
Of the woodworkers in Cambrai, of Zennor,
Of Auch, Winchester, of High Garonne.
A dream had perched him high
On a Suffolk Punch, a stallion,
And slid him off the broad back of it;
Rounding the belly, there, in that dream,
A new Columbus, looking up

He saw the splendour, ALL IN PLACE,
Saw the heavy hanging equine genitals.

Always looking up!

Into the star branches of mahogany.
Into the maple.
Into the anatomical twigs of bird on bird.
Into the stretch marks that streak

Pregnant wood with beak and talon,
Feather bowers of our aspirant skeletons –
Cradles of verdure our evolving nerves
Pirouette around but seldom glory in –
Not always on the bright side, looking up –

4

So comes the ringtail cat
When Philip walks his usual track one day:
Big as this, he gestures, his arms
Holding out, full stretch (and him
No giant of a man) a make-believe accordion,
And the banded tail, he whispers,
Huge as in the stories that are ancient.

Now you know, he says, with an animal,
An animal, mind you, you must look down,
Come to a halt. The animal
Appreciates that. The animal also looks
Courteously down. So we faced each other off.

And I murmured something to him.
The sound, they want to hear it.
Gently you breathe it out, but loud enough.

5

His hands now poised over the table cloth,
Not as in prayer, but cupping still the grain
And cool and scent and weight of trees;
Then folded they were, for to negotiate
A deal with the cat. So he murmured it:

Hallo there, old chap. I'm glad
You came back, hope you plan to stay.
My place, your place. And if
It's out of the Chihuahua you done wander,
We've rats galore for you to relish,
And plenty of water, so tuck in.
But now, if you don't mind,

I'll hie me back to my barn down there
And see what more I just might try to do,
With my chisel, for that mantis
Girl bird with a hat of antlers,
Who has moved into my imagination
Out of the stored centuries of an elm.

Of Primo Levi's Death

While I am hearing tell
Of Primo Levi's death
I see two doves, first one
And then the other fell

Buoyed up by air alone
Filling their wingspread:
Four floors down a stairwell
He threw himself, they said.

Still the coincidence grew:
Those were mourning doves,
And as the story ended –
"Nightmares hounding him . . .

Graceful imagination
By evil still tormented . . . "
Hardly having touched the ground
Back up again they flew.

5

Adagio for Diogenes

Little maple, in your tub,
Teach me (I want to say) how to resist
A sleep that stretches into me,
The careful sleep of strangers in a cabin.
First your top twigs will sprout,
No effort, a vestigal red:
Show me how to think of that.

Look at you now, with your limited
Root spread, your vermilion
Twiggery flutters. Cold sleep,
Look at you resisting it, the grip
Of a negative I feared you just might
Come to be. Look at you: thin bark
Sheathes new stems you lifted up.

As I hoist this apostrophe, no sweat,
Out of archaic dirt, you from your ballast
Draw nutrient sap for me to excogitate.
Deeper into my tub I ram it, look at you,
Airing it now, all winter wide awake.

Look at you, impavid and full
Of sparrows that seem, if I give up,
Blobs chirping, automatic, and basta.
I wish to hear the sense of those songs.
Of knot and loop a twittering thread
Thrills the web of being, does it? Their
Solos are so short, and you their perch.
Faintly those trebles delineate a fact:
"It's me today," the sparrow said.

But to resist, to let fly at bleaker
Matters, admit the Inexorable, with a mind
To joy more harsh as volume shatters
This tub in which my roots are buried –
What of that? Your contorted trunk,
Crooked growth you could not help,
Tells me not to panic when desire
Smokes me out, me, not a moment whole,
Hospitable only in small ways.

Across grime sunflowers will explode.
Sky splits with the racket of Neptune.
Hereabouts, rhythm lost, lives are shook up,
Signposts churn the blue like weathervanes,
Arteries clog, power stupefies.
Over there, little maple, what gives?
Steady in the design, a hand, are you that?
Immobile, but a fountain, mapping sky,
Flush with air, a liquid wink?

The Prostration of William Cowper

O Muse, make little of my gratitude,
It's real but only when I read your dreams.
Your intermittent whisper is my food,
But speaking for myself I starve, it seems.

Appear to me, if need be, upside down.
At least rebuke me, if I set you straight.
If on my fragmentary work you frown,
Frown only little and too late.

Me, born cracked, they say, upon this midden –
No, but ill-mixed, part ant, part dog, no shell,
I've glimpsed and sniffed in words the seed of Eden
And woofed and laboured, empty thrice, through hell.

Please do not let them kill me in the street.
Suffice it that I stumble where such people are
As make their lives, how should I say, complete
Nor ever quaked at the magnitude of a star;

For terrible motions do afflict a man;
He babbles on, no wonder, putrid enough –
I mean a mute rage rakes the also-ran
And strikes a has-been from the script of love.

Bare bones on my plate, this baked potato skin.
Take me or leave me, I will stuff them in.

Elegy for our Wilted Tigers

One beside the other, each with her other feeling
Sister to the one, their brains blended,

Two cats, one cloudy grey, the other
Gold and chocolate, scantly fed

Long years they clung to one another
"Sitting in the sun under the dove house wall".

There was no dove house. Only the hot
Underground water pipe to warm them,

Through any hard winter freeze they crouched,
Snuck up under the wall, and stole their sleep

On a bed of concrete. The chocolate one,
It pulled at the other's dug: Juliet's

Nurse in Verona, her infant Susan dead,
Would have told herself it was practical –

Sucking, and giving suck, so to stay alive.
Curious. These cats were not assimilated,

Or interesting like the cats of Possum.
They were eccentric, but from hunger dull.

What was indoors they did not care to ask –
Great bags of biscuit? In their scope

Only the crumbs mattered, strewn on the carpet,
Threadbare, muffling heeltaps in the portico.

In their hearts, horn never called to the chase:
No chase in them, no picture of plump young rat.

So they hung out, in suspense, flies with feet
Trapped in glue, still hoisting wings, their analogue,

Or people with tattoos who nurse a grievance,
Or Pompey in the ship where they hacked off his head.

Now that the grey cat has been four days gone
Into the vague terrain, or curling up to die

In the bamboo thicket, weary of it all,
I can only wonder if, or how, or when

She might have said goodbye to her friend.
Now into the steel thrusting oil

And captive air with red rear lights ahead
Need grinds me, me also adrift

Empty across limbo, I sniff out a reason
Why her scowl hurt you like a bite,

Why she never let you touch her pelt,
Why, half-shut eyelids narrowing her gaze,

She took off, quick, if you so much
As asked her tenderly for her name.

Feuilleton 8: The Solitary Welcomes

1. *Italianas in Berlin*

How very welcome, now and then,
The laughter of those ladies in the sun;
How very welcome, always, every rush
Of laughter, theirs, from the courtyard
When sunlight folded into it
Lightens the green, stealthily picks out
The tunes of ivory and rose those Maytime
Candelabras flourish, pinning flounces
Around the huge rooted chestnut tree.

For when you hear the ladies laughing
You see a laughter, welcome, lift,
Parallel, from pink and white and green;
It whirs with the electric mixer,
Plucks the cords of a double bass booming far
Behind it all; it tastes of the cream
Those ladies have been whisking up
With strawberries chopped fine
For their holiday tea time.

2. *A Hotel Foyer*

To the dog in the diagonal mirror,
The dog at the top of ten steep stairs,
Who with his long motley hair terrifies
Wolves at the foot of the stairs

And wrongly branded sheep,
Sheep wanting a fold for a night,

To the dog who looms in the flesh with gravity
When you are mounting the ninth stair,
Woof a welcome.

3. *A Benin Woman*

Should it be you she welcomes with memory
Of bronze, the Benin woman in the Metro
– Her chin so round, her jawbone swept
Back as once the blade of a ploughshare,
Now her nose with nostril grottoes,
Slanting hazel eyes –

                Welcome in return herself,
Welcome her spindly braids
                Siphoned up into a topknot
So tight the roots of hair showed their furrows
For glistening skin
To make her nutmeg skull a helmet –

Her buttoned coat, glossy pantaloons,
Eventually shoes of jet have housed
                An earthlight still in bud:

So she slaves on, her body magic
Not to be touched by these razors
Of numerals and smells and pictures –
An Africa deep underground, welcome
                As a pool in Yucatan.

4. *Historiette*

Welcome for once to the tune
Secret in Czerny's tripping drills:
Here she goes, the child –
Grasshopper
Fingertips touch
Notes in a flow of
G, for soon the sharp –
Angled sunlight prompts
Our rooftop songbird too,
And here again is France.

Welcome back, the *historiette*
And easily requisite
Opening bars of Gretchaninoff.
Sixty years on and a touch
Light as mint on her tongue
Can welcome one day back to her
The whole tune magnified
By an atmosphere, all gist –

Will her drinking cup outlive her?

Then those notes for wicked Pépé,
Haunting presence, ran huge
Down their channel, like a blade:
The act, welcome again; in a phrase
She stumbles over
Echo happens, dark nymph, with a click.
Still they knit, the skinny women.

So in her knots of pain augmented
France diversifies; as high comic

Her shriek of rage
As dry his covered well.

5. *Palmetto*

Sun gone almost down
Cloud hoods the ring of hills,
And a gentle rain – there
Troughs that groove palmetto spears
Decant small whispering worlds

Down into the knotted
Cactus heart. Welcome,
Housed in the coffee maker,
White cups, a brace of them;
Bitter drink for one alone.

Still, in the minikitchen, welcome
At the top of the stone
Curved stair, for you,
Renegade ghost, longest love,
Brimful of grit, the other cup.

Welcome, on that score, such peaks
In the heart, and coiling
Valley roads, the slopes
Regular with vines; here the *tilleul*,
Greener for dusk, growing rotund,

Welcomes a bee throng throat-singing
Halfway to honey. No gradual
Landmass, no sentiment
Stony in denial, in lungs
Puffed by mundane toil,

Can escape, again and now tomorrow
Sighs to set the unfarmed
Hill crests pulsing.
                    Welcome, shadow, sweep on:

Defang with your calm
The brute, Vacancy.
Bolt against grievance the door.

Black Saturn

From time to time
The table shook
The grandpa drummed
His fingers on it

Summer nights
Swelling pods
Heavier heavier
Older and older

The tomcat too
Him snowy ginger
Beside the grandpa
Sat and blinked

See grandpa closer
Skyblue cotton
Shirt and pants
He look so sharp

Two glittery eyes
For fighting war
And shimmery shoes
He trod so light

He peers around
Then straight ahead
Not rapt in thought
Not feeling bad

The hoary tom
With a butcher board
For furrowed forehead
Listening flicking

Ears the grandpa
Seeming equally
So-so heaves
(Forgotten why)

A sigh the table
Shook from time
To time but not
So you might notice

Whining gnats
Belabour grandpa
Spooks of ice
In a crystal ring

Some time long gone
They made a moon
What a bang that was
When it exploded

Says the grandpa
How do crystal sing
So a gnat be ice
To Tom she mew

The Counter-Missionary

Somewhere along the trail he took
A wrong fork. Front and rear,
Vegetation thickened. No machete.
No knowledge of the creole spoken
By indigenous people.

Still he could cajole them, not with talk,
But action, till he died at eighty,
Into fine cooking. How not to fear
But love their gods. In token
Whereof no peculiar church with steeple

Did he construct. He bequeathed,
Before he breathed
His last, only a tall tin stove.
No wick, no paraffin, no flame.
They loved it all the same.

On Breaking Bread with J. Alfred Prufrock

There is this thrill
    Runs like an asegai
Back through

What? It can't stop
    At the sight, only
An instant, under
    A streetlight,

Of such glistening
    Black, were they only
Legs, yes, only

    But the toning, the sheen, the muscle

And her skirt slid up
    To her hips almost,
She had to be issued,
    A most regal

Complication, the legs, so long

To be extracted,
    Through a small car door,
Where can it stop

Amor, Amor, and what,
    Dug from a tumulus
Tonight, is that look

Aglow in her crest
    Of a head, her
Mint medallion?

The Word Pavilion

A very tiny European dog, it says
In the book of roots, a dog, that's all,
Derived from *papillon*, butterfly in French.

And the pavilions are disappearing:
A dark interior where the amber glows;
A hogan housing streaky smells, body-musk
And pinyon incense; a home of goatskin,
Bakhtiars on thrones of scarlet wool,
Planning peace or revenge; even a pavilion
Odorous with linseed oil, where the spin bowler
Fits his fingertips along the stitching
Of a scuffed red ball; an airy marble hall,
Uproarious with banquets, laws, armour,
Harps and the rest of it, is disappearing too.

One pavilion stayed put, it was a tent,
A tent with a flap to keep insects out,
Impenetrable to the moth or butterfly,
Even perhaps to the tiny European dog.

They seem to disappear, nevertheless.
The road is not lost, only the real pavilions,
They vanish, one by one, the frontier forts,
Assumed attitudes, defensible positions, absolutes,
With their poles, canvas, and safety flaps,
And stones to anchor them against the wind.

Then they will be coming after you, the Prosops,
Slime-blue, some torpid, some in a frenzy
Squeaking, bubble faces eating in blank time
The air around you, Prosops, mutant faces

Of apathy once vigilance,
Of acrimony once a sweetest fellow feeling,
The pad of their paws now a duller heartbeat.

So with his music the god
Abandoned Antony. But remember
The musical children trotting along the sewer,
Beneath the road south, out of Alexandria,
They played the flute, the lute, the hand harp.

All merrily trooping through the slosh,
Their music heard above ground as the awful truth:
So the myth disappeared, the myth
Put about for the benefit of Antony,
It vanished.

                    Vulnerable Antony,
Then with his wound
Haul him up, she did, into her monument.

Let them be, the vanishing pavilions.
Others may make more of their fabric,
More of their finery than you could.
There will be remnants, surely, for someone.

And the road, even if you lost it,
The road does not lose itself in such a darkness,
The dark beginning to glow, all air
A sparkling darkness to be created
For more than horrors to inhabit,
For the old hardness that means to dance
In those bare bones.

Old Milwaukee Man's Wonders

for Donald Weismann

Not any more that lake with its cataract,
A crescent moon, afloat on it;
Not any more the brush, free of its fidget,
So an image flowers, lightly, under it.

Not that any more, nor new metal objects,
Not any intergalactic whatnot;
Nor confusion of loves, you catch your breath,
But ride on over it. Not any more,
Even, grief at the death of friends.

It is, he says, a pebble standing out in the grit.
A shadow it throws on the road. It is an ant
In the shadow, *in* it. This dear dog now
Likes to hear the cars go past, leaps up
And lies on the stone wall, listening.

                    No regrets
When they pass out of earshot,
And I am looking at this ant, how it shifts,
At this pebble, no part of me,
Going no place.

Language Learning

Never mind the early
Imitative stages: each
Blessed thought
Absorbing words as

Supplied, words
Macerated in
Emotion vaporous
With age, and thought

On "warm", mechanically
Roasting, itself soon
"A memory", garden
Speckled with monuments.

At three score plus,
Your word-world splits:
Things persist, the matching
Words are not quite yours.

You forget names,
Mango and Morandi;
You recite the alphabet,
Hoping memory will snag

On a splinter, but if
A name comes back it seems
To tiptoe out of nowhere,
Voiceless, random,

A reason to wonder,
Wonder if all things, all
Words together intend
An image of something else.

Then beware: catch
The fugitive, arrest
Memory by the moment,
To that slack muscle

Tone returns with art
And exercise, you can thwart
Memory's monkey tricks,
The words team up again.

But the things, have they
Forgotten where on earth
They put their words? Words
Now do not constitute them;

Or things retract their
Public names, and you,
You still profane
Their secret ones.

How then to hear them? Though
"Dialogue with a person who
Forgot the words"
May delight the sage,

Still they rattle
Ghostly chains,
Scare not the things
But you away, perhaps.

For the things at least
Look distinct,
Are done, happening, still
They float, they hurt

Something cruel: not certain
If they want back
Into their words
Or out –

The fresh adventure,
The brighter air.

Hotel Asia Minor

A sickly smell pervades at five
The tiny shower. Pull the plug
And from the unstable toilet stool
Bright water spilling on the floor
Might cause a gentleman to slip,
Grabbing the basin, which come loose;
But now and then the water's hot,
So praise the bathroom you have got.

The little room for sleep, oblong;
And many splotches on the walls
Betoken battles; bladdered gnats
Exploded there, attacked by towels.
But it is snug, in summer too
A nook suspended in the air;
Two windows in thick walls are square
And under one a table fits,

Place for an ashtray and a book
And elbows propping up your head;
Its shadow falls – from forty watts
A golden light licks every page.
A patio, outside, festooned
With trumpet vines that wind around
A pinewood column, fretted screen –
Ottoman origin, I suppose –

Contains, beneath a roof of slats,
A second little table. On
The tombstone chipping floor its legs
Might well be steadied by four pegs,
But it will do to scribble at –
Innocent reader, persevere,

There is no spiritual crisis here,
No opera of the intellect.

The tufa cliff behind the house
Is pierced by cavities: old graves,
Where nothing sprouts but silver doves
And tufts of green for dragonflies.
One cavity is overhung
By a rock lip, and snuck well in –
A dovecote: he who scoops the dung
Has a royal crop of aubergines.

Two benches on the patio,
Each like a long sarcophagus,
Adjoin to form the letter L;
Not marble, not upholstered, no,
What buoys them up? So hard to tell.
Yet there I lie, to catch some zees,
On stucco, prone; a groaning bus
I hearken to, the gasp of a truck

Hellbent on something, then the knock
Of donkey hoofs on cobblestones.
A magpie's chatter in the trees,
The flit of sparrows through the vines,
Desist at night, and nights are cool:
As slow plops in the water tank
Echo a starlit owlet's call –

I fold my hands with her to thank.

Envoi: An Apple Tree in Normandy

for John and Anne Willett

Did the apple tree fall down
Or was it pushed?
Boreas hopping the Channel?
Someone heavy and drunk?

Four thick fallen branches turn
A static cartwheel. At the broken
Base the buried fibres, even then,
Conduct the good. Leaves evolve

And apples in due season.
A crooked scheme of shadows
Brightens the lawn. On a fine day,
Dawn to dusk, it swivels, ah –

Hissing, two characters at loggerheads
In a sketch by Guys or Cruikshank.
The trunk, a mat of moss to perch on,
When a lookalike, yours truly, quits it,

A flycatcher flits in, the early bird,
Occupies a nook, and unimportantly
Targets, minute after minute,
Something in the air.

Selected Poems

Objects at Brampton Ash

The quick thrush cocks his head,
bunching his pectorals, halted.

Long holly shadows hone his shining claw;
you thumb its edge and grass gets grassier.

The tapered spire, at anchor in its ring
of tomb and cedar, has to quit ascending.

So you revolve in hearth-smoke's occult caves,
banished by touch of frost beading the roofs.

What increase, could these ends outlast
perpetual waste.

At Porthcothan

A speck of dark at low tide on the tideline,
It could not be identified as any known thing,
Until, as one approached, a neck was clear
(It is agreed that logs, or cans, are neckless),
And then a body, over which the neck stood
Curved like a questionmark, emerged
As oval, and the whole shape was crouching
Helpless in a small pool the sea had left.

The oval body, with green sheen as of pollen
Shading off into the black plumage, and the neck
Surmounted by the tiny wide-eyed head,
Were not without beauty. The head was moving,

So like a cobra it seemed rash to offer
An introductory finger to the long hooked bill
Stabbing the air. Danger had so
Sharpened what intelligence the bird possessed,
It seemed to pierce the mind of the observer.
In fact we were afraid, yes afraid of each other.

Finally though I picked it up and took it
To a quiet side-bay where dogs were rarer.
Here the shag sat, happy in the sun,
Perched on a slab of rock where a pool was,
In which I caught five fish for it
With a pocketknife, a handkerchief
And a plunging forefinger. But at six o'clock
It left the rock and waddled off seaward.

Though breakers came in high and curling
It straddled them, bouncing, buoyant,
Borne along the sealine sideways, with head up,
Slithering across the bay's whole width, and then
Drifted ashore again, to scuttle flapping
With webbed feet flat like a Saturday banker's
To shelter on a level rock. Here it studied,
With the air of one of whom something is expected,
The turbulent Atlantic slowly rising.
What could I do but leave it meditating?

Early next morning, on the bay's north side,
I found it cuddled under the cliff. The tide
Was low again. What hungry darkness
Had driven so the dark young shag to shelter?
It did not resist when I picked it up.
Something had squeezed the cobra out of it.

I took it to a cave where the sun shone in,
Then caught two fish. It opened one green eye,
And then another. But though I cut
The fish into portions, presenting these
To the bill's hooked tip, it only shook its head.
Noon came. The shag slept in the cave. At two
I hurried back. The shag was stone dead,
With its fine glossy head laid back a little
Over the left shoulder, and a few flies
Were pestering its throat and the fish scraps
Now unlikely to get eaten.

                  Ten minutes perhaps
I sat there, then carried it up the cliff path
And across the headland to a neighbouring cove
Where oystercatchers and hawks flew and far
Far below in loose heaps small timber lay, tickled
By a thin finger of sea. There I flung the shag,
For in some such place, I thought,
Such bodies best belong, far from bathers, among
The elements that compose and decompose them,
Unconscious, strange to freedom, but perceptible
Through narrow slits that score the skin of things.

Or perhaps (for I could not see the body falling)
A hand rose out of air and plucked the corpse
From its arc and took it, warm still,
To some safer place and concealed it there,
Quite unobtrusively, but sure, but sure.

Edward Lear in February

Since last September I've been trying to describe
two moonstone hills,
and an ochre mountain, by candlelight, behind.
But a lizard has been sick into the ink,
a cat keeps clawing at me, you should see my face,
I'm too intent to dodge.

Out of the corner of my eye,
an old man (he's putting almonds into a bag)
stoops in sunlight, closer than the hills.
But all the time these bats flick at me
and plop, like foetuses, all over the blotting paper.
Someone began playing a gong outside, once.
I liked that, it helped; but in a flash
neighbours were pelting him with their slippers and
    things,
bits of coke and old railway timetables.

I have come unstuck in this cellar. Help.
Pacing up and down in my own shadow
has stopped me liking the weight it falls from.
That lizard looks like being sick again. The owls
have built a stinking nest on the Eighteenth Century.

So much for two moonstone hills,
ochre mountain, old man
cramming all those almonds into a bag.

The Thousand Things

Dry vine leaves burn in an angle of the wall.
Dry vine leaves and a sheet of paper, overhung
by the green vine.
From an open grate in an angle of the wall
dry vine leaves and dead flies send smoke up
into the green vine where grape clusters go
ignored by lizards. Dry vine leaves
and a few dead flies on fire
and a Spanish toffee spat
into an angle of the wall
make a smell that calls to mind
the thousand things. Dead flies go,
paper curls and flares,
Spanish toffee sizzles and the smell
has soon gone over the wall.

A naked child jumps over the threshold,
waving a green spray of leaves of vine.

Male Torso

Before I woke, the customed thews
Alighted on strangeness.
Crammed over booms of vine,
The once buxom canvas quilled.

From his hot nest, before I woke,
The snowgoose flew, in skyward rings;
And funnelled air that filled my mouth
Rang with his wingbeat.

The customed eyes, before I woke, were glass;
A bleating queen whose legs were sheaths
Of hammered moon fed swill to pigs;
With needle oars they swept her bark

Through floes of starfruit, dolphins cutting
Under her eyelid's bow blue arcs in air;
And the beat of their oars like drums
Fanned my hushabye head.

Before I woke, no savour was;
But three birds sang that song they piped as girls,
Of sweetness, golden-rinded, and the fountaintree,
For mortal grapes cooled in my hands.

Then down the quartz-walled galleries of ears I coiled,
Before I woke; cymbals clashing sliced their hill,
And there with bulls my skew-wigged mother trod
Her crocus dance around its axle;

Counterwheeling Horn and Bear
Shared in her coronal the thud of fingertips of flutes,
Until my customed silence dipped and rose,
And gall was mine and darkness was.

I live now in a hutch of mud,
Without a floor, nailed by the sun,
Now for the interminable writhing sea
A fair food housed in roofless marble.

But if I wake to sniff the air of clustered stars,
I'm clothed in dew, for babes to drink,
The snowgoose moors her nest on light,
And the small horned worms walk high with hope.

News from Norwood

Professor Palamedes darts down Westow Street.
Nothing explains how he avoids
Colliding with mutton, plastics, pianos.
Professor Palamedes, darting down Westow Street,
Tunnels through petrol fumes and tundra;
Rhomboid oysterbeds under his rubbers,
Sparrows and sandwiches scatter before him.

Where is he going, Professor Palamedes?
It's well past three. What has he forgotten?
What can he have forgotten, Professor Palamedes,
Who stood with Agur by Solomon's elbow,
Who flogged the sea, full of nymphs and sheep,
Whom meat moods or helpful harmonies do not perplex?

Let us say he is going toward the stranger.
Again: he is going toward the stranger.
No matter who. The stranger. Who showed his face.
Who showed his face over Solomon's shoulder;
Who saw at Salamis, as planks buckled and the nymphs
Cheered, how sheep just went on cropping grass,
Side by side, to a tinkling of bells.

Climbing a Pebble

What did it mean (I ask myself), to climb a pebble.
From the head of a boy depends a very thin cloud.
A red speck shifting on the Roman Campagna.
This sea-rubbed pebble has no cleft for toes.

It is simple, the ant said (my Nares and Keats).
You start low down, with caution. You need not
Slash your soles for lime like medieval Swiss.
No, but with spread arms, easing up, imperceptibly
Colluding with the air's inverted avalanche.
This cushions, O, the aching spine.

A very thin cloud is falling from the sky.
A shot, a shifting robe of crimson,
Whiffs of powder in the wind –
The sidelong buffet slams. And still you cling,
Still easing upward; giant glades, they creaked and shone,
Fresh mown, now small below – you do not smell them.

And you begin to know what it can mean,
Climbing a pebble. The paradise bird
Drops, dies, with beak fixed in the ground.
An urchin made off with its cloudthin tail.
A cardinal, with footmen to load his fowling pieces,
Peppers Italian larks a glass held spellbound.

The glass was tied to an owl, the owl to a stick.
I struck the pebble, digging, as the sun went up.

Five Psalms of Common Man

'Je n'aime pas le dimanche'

1

Whisky whipping g-string Jaguar megaton
sometimes a 'purely rational human being'

it's me they tell of yonder sea devoid of amber
it's me they tell of column and haunting song

noncommittal me my mumble eaten
by the explosions of clocks and winds without routine

not fountains not millennia of light inextinguishable
ebbing through column and throat with its
   wombwombwomb

come my pet my demagogue excruciate me watching
yonder fountain douse the yolky dunes

2

The creatures of coal have looked for you all over;
the creatures of tea heard a snatch of song, it was not you.

The creatures of smoke have looked for you all over;
the creatures of tar saw a tree, it was not you.

The hand was not you, nor the hairy ear;
the belly was not you, nor the anklebone.

The eyeball was not you. Tongue and teeth
and jawbone were not you. The creatures of hair

have looked for you all over; the creatures of snow
touched a locked door, it was not you.

The creatures of paper have looked for you all over;
the creatures of steel smelled thick wallets, it was not you.

These creatures wanted to be free to look for you;
and all the time you looked to be free of their want for you.

3

W.N.P. Barbellion (pseudonymous)
March 1915
sees 'on the top of an empty omnibus
a little heap of dirty used-up bus tickets
collected by chance in the corner'

felt sick
the number of persons
the number of miles
the number of buses

at all times
the number of voices
the number of voices not speaking to one another
perplexity without suprise

Avenues Madison Shaftesbury Opéra
the number of heart beats
without number

the sick one is he on whom his desire advances asking
        why
the sick one is he who has begun all over again
not wanting not
'waiting that hour which ripens to their doom'

He speaks (Adolf Eichmann April 1961)
'in starchy, clerkish language
full of abstractions
pedantry
euphemism'

4

My blind wife kicking in her flesh of flies.
My blind wife in her ring of ribs beating me flat.
But no shard of keg shall cool my last bones.

The flies were dancing in their ring.
Their ring was dancing in the flies.
The ring desired by the nature of flies.

Stomach eyes packing it all in tight.
Knotted wings kicking in a glue film.
Ghosted in glue was the nature of eyes.

Revolt severe if sieved for its ghost of motive.
Air without motive rubbing in the arid throat.
My blind wife I warm to the coolness of bones.

Order imagined against fear is not order.
Saith man. Fear imagined against order
only negates or does not negate existing order.
Out of a rumbling of hollows an order is born
to negate another existing order of fear.

Nights broken before they end, interrupting
the millennia of my vigilance, saith man.
The nights of past time never slept to the end
re-enact themselves in the existing order of fear.

Another order of fear is chaos.
Images of chaos variously coordinated
by disparate imaginations accord or do not accord
to their seasons in time enacting the indeterminations.
The orders revolve in the ring or do not evolve.

The orders revolve as improvisations against fear,
changed images of chaos. Without fear, nothing.
Let me, saith man, take another look at the sea again.
And in his ear begin the rumblings of keels again.

Cabal of Cat and Mouse

He has a way, the cat, who sits
on the short grass in lamplight.
Him you could appreciate, and more –
how the musky night fits him,
like a glove; how he adapts down there,
below boughs, to his velvet arena.

His, for playing in. A shadow
plodding past his white paws
could be a swad of anything;
except that, as it bolts, he retrieves
and has tenderly couched it,
and must unroll alongside, loving.

His paws dab and pat at it; his
austere head swivels at an angle
to the barrel neck. Prone, he eyes
its minutest move; his haunch relaxing
parades tolerance, for the pose entreats
doubly to play – it is energy

involved, if you like, in a tacit exchange
of selves, as the cat flares up again,
and has seized what he seizes.
And acts proud, does a dance, for it is
his appetite puts all the mouse into a mouse;
the avid mouse, untameable,

bound by so being to concur,
in his bones, with the procedure.
Even the end cannot cancel that.
The shift from play to kill, measured,
is not advertised. He has applied
a reserved gram of tooth power,

to raise this glibbering curt squeal
at last, and now glassily gazes down.
Plunged, barked as if punched,
and has axed his agitator. You heard
soon the headbones crunch; and you shrank,
the spine exploding like a tower in air.

The Child at the Piano

The child at the piano
plinking, planking, plonks.
I stare and stare. Twigs
angle the air with green outside.

Handfuls of notes, all happening at once,
her tunes do not occur; on their backs
round they whizz like stunned wasps; contour
would crush that kind of mass.

Telescoping flukes and faults, their
tenuous terrain dislocates
no spheres I know of. Her index rebounding
off high   C beckons no hell boulder
up.

The heroics, fatuous, ordain yet
this act's assumption of her whole element.
Boughs of sound swoop through the room,
happily, for her to swing from.

So I call my thought's bluff. My thumb
struts down the keys, too, pings
to her plonks, on both white and black notes,
while the green air outside lets us be.

January 1919

What if I know, Liebknecht, who shot you dead.
Tiergarten trees unroll
staggering shadow, in spite of it all.
I am among the leaves; the inevitable
voices
have nothing left to say, the holed head
bleeding across a heap of progressive magazines;
torn from your face,
trees that turned around,
we do not sanctify the land with our wandering.
Look upon our children, they are mutilated.

Disturbing the Tarantula

The door a maze
of shadow, peach leaves
veining its wood colour,

and cobwebs broken
breathing ah ah
as it is pushed open –

two hands
at a ladder shook
free the tarantula, it slid

black and fizzing to a rung
above eye-level,
knees jack knives,

a high-jumper's, bat mouth
slit grinning
into the fur belly –

helpful: peaches
out there, they keep growing
rounder and rounder

on branches wheeled low
by their weight over
roasted grass blades; sun

and moon, also, evolve
round this mountain
terrace, wrinkling now

with deadly green
emotion: All things
are here, monstrous convulsed

rose (don't anyone
dare come), sounding through
our caves, I hear them.

Navajo Children,
Canyon de Chelly, Arizona

You sprouted from sand,
running, stopping, running;
beyond you tall red
tons of rock rested
on the feathery tamarisk.

Torn jeans, T-shirts
lope and skip, toes drum
and you're coming
full tilt
for the lollipops,

hopefully
arrive, daren't
look, for our stares
(your noses dribble)
prove too rude

in your silence,
can't break, either,
your upturned
monkey faces into smiles.
It's no joke,

as you grope
up, up
to the driver's door, take
them reverently, the
lollipops –

your smallest, too small,
waited three
paces back, shuffling,
then provided,
evidently

by a sister on tiptoe who
takes his hand, helps
unwrap the sugar totem.
And we are swept
on, bouncing,

look back,
seeing walls
dwarf you. But how
could you get any
more thin, small, far.

For a Junior School Poetry Book

The mothers are waiting in the yard.
Here come the children, fresh from school.
The mothers are wearing rumpled skirts.
What prim mouths, what wrinkly cheeks.
The children swirl through the air to them,
trailing satchels and a smell of chalk.

The children are waiting in the yard.
The mothers come stumbling out of school.
The children stare primly at them,
lace their shoes, pat their heads.
The mothers swirl through the air to cars.
The children crossly drive them home.

The mothers are coming
The children are waiting.
The mothers had eyes that see
boiled eggs, wool, dung and bed.
The children have eyes that saw
owl and mountain and little mole.

The Ancestors

When they come, we begin to go;
it's the ancestors,
they walk into the warm rooms,

eye our women and food, hear out
the good words. Then for words
and rooms we no more exist,

once the ancestors have come,
than a little dust on a vase,
than the breath wasted.

How do they come? They make no
parade of moans and winds;
they borrow no fears, none.

I am persuaded they have come
by the strength of shoes,
by the one shirt extra,

but if most by the bloody love
my shoes and my shirt need
to be seen that way,

I tell myself this is a thing
they'd far better not know,
who have lost the knack,

and only accuse, by the malice
they march us out with, from one
to the next lost place.

Old Bottles

It must have been long
I lay awake,
listening to the shouts
of children in the wood.
It was no trouble, to be awake;
not to know
if that was what I was.

But I had to buy
old bottles, barter
for steerage, candles too,
each stamped with my name.
It was hurry hurry
racing the factory canal toward
the town of the kangaroo.

Up the street I came
across a knot of dead boys.
In the room with a flying bird
on practising my notes
I found its lingo;
my body knew
those torsions of the cat.

She came by, that girl,
she said it's to you, to you
I tell what they are doing
in South Greece and Germany.
My parents killed, brother gone,
They'll read this letter, I'll
not be here, you do not understand.

In my striped pyjamas
I was not dressed for the journey.
I changed into padded zip
jacket, boots, canvas trousers,
my pockets bulged with the bottles,
I was carrying the candles,
and I ran and I ran.

Sanity

After bolting my supper,
    eggs, sausages, bacon and chips,
I see this photograph in the paper:
    it is a crowd of ordinary people,
the Jew cocking his thatched head, the old
    vocal woman, the mechanic.

Two hold the middle of the picture:
    a young man, whose face, head-on,
has the symmetry of a dark Ajax;
    a young woman, hair anyhow,
high cheekbones, the lips parting,
    her remote eyes look straight at you.

They are walking beneath many banners.
    These they uphold casually.
The whole crowd is coming at you.
    I walk across the room, for the first time
can raise my face to the black trees,
    a silver sky of Spring.

Dangers of Waking

Waking has dangers. When children
stride into the room, one by one, with reports
and messages, you shout and roll over;
a slamming of doors, a sound of breaking.

Like a friend you meet – what he
confides to you, you, with your empty look,
turn against him: enmity of others
who can confide nothing to anyone.
They were always the aliens,

ignored or savaged by racier children,
regretfully refused a place
in useful professions. Desirable
dead or mute or not at all,
soon every sound they heard,

voices or wheels or waters,
or wind in the barbed wires,
was the sound of a key turning in a lock.
But these dangers of waking –
well, you'll roll over, shout, do nothing,

as when the children strode in,
one by one, like Greek messengers,
to declare the killing of this or that
man, thousand, million
on the good green sward.

Itinerary for the Apparent Double

With you the lane winds uphill,
by day, hatching schemes;
by night, cockshut memory overhauls
your brooding mobile mind.

It steepens for you, on splay claws,
feeling the weight of eggs not engendered yet;
up the incline a lost day
floats its faint rose of shadows.

It is dark from the hill's foot to halfway up.
Boys with stones have smashed the bulbs; some shinned
corkscrewing up the posts, to rob them, furtively.
Morgue of maidenhead, nigredo, always foots the hill.

Here, for girls, black men come jumping
big from the ditch with naked choppers.
The mewing of owls armours them as they bolt
with goosepimples and their foretaste of moans on beds.

Yet with you the path can be picked out
from the furrow of hushed and curving space
dividing oak bough from oak bough on either side.
On the upturned face a breath of cloud and two stars.

All for you, who edge forward into the dark,
who have no mind to harp on foreterror,
trust these rounds of light, crossribbed by shade,
to be bodies, nameable, loafing against the fence.

Among them you mount the curve to the one lamp.
Here foliage hoards the spray of beams;
myriads of leaves have multiplied occult dawns.
So the beetle steals through moss in the summer night,

locked in his portable house, which he cannot enter,
and is overwhelmed by the cresting forests of chrysoprase.
You'd find it harder going, to their Cold Mountain;
always the snow cone with its ice flanks recedes,

brands in muscle the black joy of the primal motions –
mystery of effort, this seeming barely to move,
till the body, twice-born, swells with tender power,
raging afresh to expel the last stride.

It might be something, to have lived like this,
with a vacant air, behind those blessed eggs.
Yet you crossed the ridge. You have begun to drop,
free, from the zone of calm that is gorged with nothing.

Or does another day convict by the death of so many,
the slope sucking you under as you run to the choked town,
through shrieks of birds that flash in the sun like axes?
What pain you have to bring, from ignorance, always.

You flail the earth with it, you track the sun's wheel,
either way, up or down, following everywhere the hill;
the child of ashes has it for a spoon;
it domed the round Iberian tomb before Carthage came.

So you are continuous, and might have been noble;
but you will forget and I forget what you have forgotten:
how deep the hill shines under its shade of tall trees,
and when no stars come, goes to them darkly upward.

An Englishman in Texas

for Donald Hall

First he sees the sky. It is the one thing
not making as if to move. Far south
its blue excites the long spine
of hills. To fetch him
home from that higher tangle
could take years.

Coombs below those hills detain him. Sheep jaws
munch on berries which now ripen through
low thickets. A creek appears,
whose yellow weed foam
ephemerids populate.
Limestone belts

polished by bursts of huge rain will occur,
across trails leading him from nowhere
to nowhere. The lizard gapes
beneath a boulder,
and admits, magenta-mouthed,
the baked air

crusting some inveterate scarab. Twirl
of cardinal bird song and blue jay's
retch sculpt on space distincter
verges. Heat becomes
inhabitable, fresh fanned
from their throats.

His haze diminishes, too, when one roof
of rusting tin has topped a hollow,
as if its apparition –
manhandled – had let
at last the estranged eye in
on something.

It hardly exists. Has stuck it out by
a mere stronger irrelevance than
the horned goat skull's candid gaze
levelled at his gaze
across curly miles of scrub.
Prickly pear

looks like a telling friend for time's cripple.
Dwarf cedars thronging undulations
balk grass and buckwheat between
those hills and his place;
so each dawn, like milk, they leave
his new wish

to be present, now, to drop character,
its greed for old presences, its dirt
fruiting demi-selves in groves.
Yet there still he prods
that suture of hill and sky
for ways through . . .

Help him, tall shades, Wallace and Westfall, whose
addresses, inconspicuously,
changed as men flocked round and round
your cockeyed cabins,
bleating and sad, agog at
the gun's wit.

Or do not help him. But let him move once,
free, of himself, into some few things.
Sky, after all, meets nothing.
And with my snake axe
I'll trudge to meet him, should he come
without you.

Three Microzoic Nonsonnets

for Hans Vogt

1

Failing: to sit
by the knotted hands
            the night through,

    all
                meaningless, as
the back of words, the black
cream of moments –

        then, on the feet,
to approach
                a door, before switching
    off,

            to put straight
a picture on the wall, the hand
        opens . . .

2

Then Goethe, he
says: The old story –
                  sea-bed (from

    this
              height down upon
Weimar), the whales playing,
    villages now;

    what thought of us,
our molluscs,
              had the sea-mew then; yet,
    think,

              hear him cross
again this mountain, his wingbeat
    not far.

3

    . . . vines, thick with fruit,
moons of pollen &
              the wild rose

    cling,
              I make them, to
the archivolts; lion,
    cathedral snail,

                    camel, my loves
            make in me
                            a room, growing; as light
                swells,

                        propels all
            night old ribby shadows up red
                    curtains.

Avebury: The Temple

What these stones are,
stone by stone,
their circle, the road
bisecting it, and the heavy
green earthwork

Night here, gradual stars,
the dew keeps rising
in a mist till the blue
and dark beeches go
for another time another green

We sleep under a mountainous
parsley stick, its rosettes and fans
catching the dew light, and darkening
with the dreams we do not have

All night a murmur and the feet
freezing soundlessly, sleeping bags
damp, not with the tears we do not shed

And at dawn we are walking
under the sweet lime trees, we climb
a gatepost of granite and sit up there

We gaze for horsemen to come,
girls with bacon,
and among grasses for the small flowers,
the far stones touching a remoteness
which is our remoteness, stones
we ask nothing of, as they are revealed

We are revealed in our hands
holding other hands

For once not scared they will come
up the road,
others who do not know what this night is,
who do not care what comes
when the night goes, the night goes

Merope

Don't let me
chase
the big stone
down the mountain

your laughter
wells
here,
little spring.

Birth of Venus

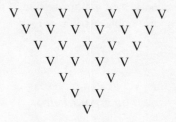

Victoriana

In the gardens of Windsor Castle
walks a philosophic owl;
wingtips clasped over his coccyx,
stooped he stalks, pondering much.

Meanwhile the moon puts pale fire
in the turrets of Windsor Castle:
shut windows halt its gleam,
the queen is pulling her boots on.

The moon is evident also
on the buttocks of stallions grazing,
in the lake without any holes,
in the blood that drips from the owl.

For certainly blood drips down
the philosophic owl:
he leaves a pool on the turf,
wherever he stops to think.

Now the queen comes riding, sag-jawed,
down the long moonlit avenue;
her dead prince gallops beside her
on a very noble ostrich.

The Armadillos

You suddenly woke and saw
on the bedroom hearth an apple green
puddle of moonlight. It was the armadillo,
sitting on top of the chimney, put it there;
with his long snout for a siphon, I suppose.

More often the armadillos
perch in the trees. They stare
at each other, count the rings
which buckle them in; or –
they discuss things.

Don't fall, Harriet! Arthur, don't fall!
We can't help it if the armadillos
drop like bombs and catch only
in the lower branches with their claws.
Falling like that, they can't be lonely.

Winters, they leave the trees and trundle
to the end of the valley. In twos and fours
they cluster there and comfort each other.
The frost feels them under their bucklers;
they taste it happening in their jaws.

But in the trees where they build hides
of cardboard boxes and paper bags,
their main concern is believing summer.
For my friends broken by special committees
I hang out armadillo flags.

They run fast and go underground
where silence is, for sending signals.
Or they climb to the tops of telephone poles
and jam the exchanges of political assholes
with the terrible sound of knitting.

If you wake again, do not scare,
but wonder at the armadillos;
they'll be watching us from up there,
winking their neat eyes, arranging their faces,
hoping that something shows.

Bonnard

Does the body rest against his eye, the cool
changing its colours: rose, purple, silver
framed in a door, the enamel of a bath

their life the elements dream through,
figures all facing at different angles
do not touch, they include one another –

dwelling on a thing, the eye feeds its boutons
energy sprayed from a few coordinates: loaf & horse,
each its own dimension in the starred dream

shields the colours! blue skins,
cocooned girl's crotch, or aloof apple,
a buffoon child, flowers in a bowl

& her face everywhere, turning from a cup
to smile with a mouth like a slice
of baby watermelon, celestial clown girl

or bored, sprawling bare on a rumpled bed,
brown arm thrown across her ribs,
the left hand tilting a small breast –

but where the skin starts it is the idyll
playing out any boundary to scan
throbbing ascensions in the space around,

street dappled with skirts & metal,
woodland blue with edible branches,
crimson billow of a kitchen cloth

it is where the dogs do battle,
canaries roast in evacuated rooms,
the history-makers unload their dead,

hack it to pieces. To pick it up again,
restore it, whole, a lifetime on fingertips
grinding a rainbow from the ignorant dew.

Found Poem with Grafts 1866

To the north-east
　　is the park of Mousseaux.
The Baths & Gardens of Tivoli
　　& the slaughter-house du Moule must be seen.
Tivoli, near the Chausée d'Antin
　　contains forty acres of ground.
It is quite equal to your Vauxhall by night
　　& is much superior in daylight.

But who is the man in the rusty black shapeless felt hat
　　pointing south-west?

The walks are ornamented
　　with roses honeysuckles & orange trees.
Amid the copses are seen
　　rope dancers & groups riding at the ring or playing at shuttlecock.
All around are arbours filled with people
　　enjoying the sight of the various amusements.
There is in the middle of the garden a theatre
　　on which two hundred couple might dance at the same time.
There are also artificial mounts from which people descend
　　in a species of car with incredible velocity.

But who stands in the huge overcoat that had once been brown
　　& is now stained with large green patches?
Who is this in the trousers that are too short,
　　revealing blue socks?

There are many canals
　　in which the public amuse themselves in boats.
In the evening
　　the illumination presents a lively spectacle.
All sorts of dances
　　commence then,

& after the vocal & instrumental concert the evening concludes
    with the exhibition of splendid fireworks.

Is he not the man who cooks
    hideous mud in the Rue Beautreillis?
Who says: The day will come
    when a single original carrot shall be pregnant with revolution,
Whose wallpaper groans with addresses in the childish script
    of nudes he throws downstairs cursing through his teeth?
And I am aglow, he says,
    with all the hues of the infinite.

The Children at Longboat Key

We have gone to the sea at evening.
We float over waves in a rubber tyre.
Your legs are glistening your hair is wet.
My shoulders are cool I hear the ripples.

Orange cloud swells over a thin black line.
We gaze at the water wheeling with rainbows.
We lean back with upturned faces.
Your hair hangs down it darkens the water.

We are floating out to sea we are happy.
On the far white sand are two black dots.
White sand curves a warm banana.
A swept a sharp banana a sword.

We see the two black dots are waving.
Bigger it grows all the sea around us.
They wave and shout we wave and wriggle.
We beat the sea with our feet and hands.

It is a very old man and a very old woman.
Far off he is jumping on the hard sand.
Far off she is brandishing a parasol.
He wears a black hat and she white stockings.

We have ridden the billows and watch the foam.
Soft crystals cling and spit on the rubber.
There are two voices shouting and mixing.
We stand in the water we feel its pull.

It is pulling your knees and you go under.
I catch your feet it is hauling you away.
The little old people walk toward us.
The sand nudges between our toes.

His black hat rim sits level over his eyes.
Her white stockings cover two sticks.
They are saying to us their big worries.
They make their hands go up and down.

We hear the voices we hold the tyre.
Its cool ring slaps to the sand between us.
They walk away in their twiggy skins.
The shrunken faces will speak no more.

They meant it well the old people.
The sea pounds the beach behind us.
Its blue roar begins like a shiver.
We watch them vanish into thin air.

Shoreham Walk

We walked
up through the wood
nettles & oak
a dark green

fall of light
leading us
past soft
erect wheat

then the white
potato flowers
& flints, a few
rusty can tops

it is the shining
June day, warm
as seldom
in our country

on our skin
a south wind
silver barley ears
are swaying

swaying us
& a lark
less visible than
the flower, blue

big, no bigger
than your pupil
under crusty
oaks again, ferns

they smell of salt
curved seawaves
& a place
we found

called the kingdom
of children
you said, because
nobody frowns

as you climbed
vanishing up
a giant beech, red
as old blood

tall as the sky,
so many strong
branches it
was easy

In Balthazar's Village

Voices in the night
    voices below begin
        wind rising orderless too
rumbles & howls

upstairs a silver light
    falls
        on collected rocks
& new maroon espadrilles

in another room
      Rampal's flute is
            Bach who breathes for these
elementary propositions

odd as it is to care
      anyhow for things
            their mass & contour
& all beginnings

A Cart with Apples

In the blue shadow
alone with its rose
and full of fields
round ones and yellow ones
an apple stands

a blue apple stands
in the field of yellow
alone with its cart
and round of roses
full ones and shadow ones

and full of yellow
the shadow stands
alone with an apple
a rose one a round one
in a blue field

and in the apple shadows
blue ones and yellow ones
a cart stands
alone with its field
and full of rounds

but in the field of roses
and full of apples
yellow ones and round ones
a blue cart stands
alone with its shadow

Petrarch's Country

This peak infuriating the winds
This valley fluting down the foothills
These crabby oaks & soon apple trees & blue grape

At the valley's other end a slope of roofs
This maze long abandoned by the tinkling animals
Old stone room inhaling all the winds

Antique prayer book this decrepit bible
Black dented bowler with a cracked brim
A lexicon of place names coming to pieces

Dead or alive someone forgot the sunday trappings
But the bowler fits I clamp it on my head
Under this peak a thousand weathers flow from

Books in hand & looking solemn enter the Café Pons
Now my full glass of wine I raise for silence
Now I drink to all the winds

Snake Rock

Tall snake without strut or buttress
snake which talks in the rhythms of chemicals
snake with legs

tell me where the spyholes are
come between my sheets and just be yourself
snake with two breasts which look at me

snake with hair and very tender armpits
show me the moon
show me the moon or must I split your skull
tell me

tell me animal with fruits
animal of cellulose and lignin come into my house
animal with leaves
cambium animal come into my house

animal which sucks minerals out of the dirt
tell me animal drinking the sun
dead centered animal shaping sugar into wood

drinking lakes also towering flower
tell me how you can change the sun into yourself
flower with a snout
rock with claws come into my kitchen
tell me how you can cook the air and crunch its bones

flower with fur
flower with padded feet smelling of incense
snake who stands in the suchness of silence
come to my table of wood and wickerwork

flower with white teeth
calcium flower teach me the revolution
rock with jaws which bite the flies and all flesh
tell me tell me the rain

snake with a wet nose tell me the lightning
tree which snorts and twitches
umbel snoozing with bristles of soft wire

flower which runs across the street suddenly
tell me how you die
tell me how you die without having to think of it.

Mandelstam to Gumilev, 1920

The word, you said, stars in terror of it
Clung to the moon; eagles folded their wings;
Men ringed it with number, dreading its radiance.

Our sounds, woven of that radiance, were sacred,
You said – but now what a stink of dead words:
Dead bees, old hive deserted.

So take from me, I ask you, for the joy of it,
A drop of sun, a drop of honey: this
Persephone's bees ordain that we should do.

There's no unmooring the same boat twice over.
Fur-shod shadow, certain things not a soul can hear,
Or overcome – the fear we live in, thick forest.

What's left to us? Only kisses,
Little bees, all shaggy, in their hives;
They fly into the open – their flight is death.

Night, forest of glass, the space they swarm through.
Taygetos, mountain forest, there they are born, bees
That feed on moments, honeyflower, and mint.

So take this gift, for the joy of it, this
Necklace, unassuming, made of dead bees:
They wove the honey, wove it back to sunlight.

Holy Cow

No, you never give us
a thought. Indifferent, down
to your codes imprinted
in fractions of mud, or up,
for that matter, to your commotions
calving new stars.

How long
and still entranced we are
by your surprises, we
believe you a body, perfect somehow
as a woman racked
with love, haloed by
her own heat, but offered, as it goes,
to any takers, you made
each brace of shadows twist
and shake.

Believing also
our bodies different
from yours, we were lost
in whatever thoughts
we robed you with. White
on the mountain, rivers the swish
of your tail, laughing harsh madame, free
with your earthquake favours, bellowing
death-songs we have sought
strange means to dominate you:
bridges, violins.

Naked
you might have appeared
to the old hunters. Should
I wear my shoes because
their masks and antlers,
fantastic forms invented
to contradict your moo, sprang into space
not without hope of wringing
from your bloody udder
drop by drop the pure milk?

In strawberry light
dances and sorcerers
rose from slime to outwit you.
Wise men watching the sea
chewed the lightning bolt. Cultures
built of their bones
crystallized
in tongues, in architectures, but
the great dome of imagined
destiny sat
capping the dreams that sweated
from spinal column and skull
our deadly chemicals.

Now, song, where
shall we go? No more to suppose
we can arrive at any
complete explanation; possibly
to live in truth apart
from paroxysms of the One; we have
a place in mind
offers the grip
to strip off not her hide
but the inedible crusts caking her,
their weight the imponderables
of history:

so like a moon her variety
sank, her wholeness
we instructed
in our oblivions, the clenched fist,
the frightened man's
mindless standard, death camp, swollen
the veins of orators convulsing
her whims into purpose.

Do not go back
to the swamp where, row on row,
the idols point. Rather to her,
at sixteen asking me
in the ice-cream parlour
how many dips, then dishing them out
with a flash of banded teeth. To someone
reading near dawn at some
ramshackle desk, aware
of the light reflected shaping itself
on a stone or piece
of an apple.

Go where I cannot,
anywhere the animals
are punished, with iron whips,
for our iniquities, and stop
voracity's fictions,
vengeance in its
continuous gathering
momentum, stop them
with a glimpse of her radiant
free
ongoing creation.

Also go to me,
who am answerable,
but walk a street through ruin
without so much
as the faint torchlight
of dejection.

Briefcase History

This briefcase was made on the Baltic coast
in 1946
some prize pig was flayed for the leather
metal stripped from a seaplane
silk for the stitching picked from parachute cord

People say where did you get that singular briefcase
and then I notice it
people ask how much did it cost
and when I say fifty cigarettes not many understand
once the leather was flying wrapped
around seaplane fuel tanks the space between
wadded with two inches of rubber
this briefcase might stop a bullet I wonder

For twenty-five years I have carried in it
books of poems battered or new
cosmic mountain notebooks plays with broken spines
bread and cheese a visiting card from Bratislava
and a pliable cranny for anything to be pocketed
at the last moment

The handle ribbed with stitches of parachute silk
anchored by clasps of seaplane metal
is worn shiny and dark with sweat
the whole thing has an unspeakable grey colour
running a fingertip over a surface
leprous one might say
various tones of grey flickering mould green
the scored leather looks to me like the footsole
of an old aborigine bowman earth in a space photo
nerve webs of a bat's wing

The two side pockets have their seams intact
two straps happily slip through buckles and hold there

Furthermore this briefcase has contained
a dynasty of shirts mostly now extinct nothing to declare
my Venus relics old stones believed
animal figures carved back of beyond in France

Everywhere
this briefcase has been with me somehow
I find reason to celebrate it today

Briefcase helping friend
ploughshare beaten from the sword
briefcase bag of tricks peaceful seaplane spirit
ocean wanderer
you have never contained an explosive device
never have you contained an explosive device
yet

Opoponax

A blue field for summer
Rib curve the dotted lines of lavender
Discontinuous flesh beating a signal out
And a man
Lifts a heart on his knife point
High

Possibly
He was hunting
He could be sacrificing
A squirt of cloud mixed in slow time
Would you believe it
With peace
It comes in a little bottle

In a little bottle
Knife in hand
A man stooped now he turns his terror
Like a fruit in the market
Palpitation of quanta
Like bomb bursts the line of lavender tufts

Now the tin cap sits tight
Rubber bung beneath
So the flashing knife will split
Memory down the middle
Mist of dawn on roofs multiform mask of cities
Moist chasm of spit and smells
Remembers the man

Now he strikes and again
But with five hundred baskets
Of flowers on its arms
Dew is calling out the names and prices
In a little bottle

Mountain throbs with rockfall
All its years at any moment
Distilled at a touch
On a fingertip fathoming the knife gash
Might balance or be crushed
Such crystal stars
Vast infolded systems
Index of man

Tenderness
And a great wet shroud
Catching the yellow blood of lavender

Extract the years of carnage
Touch your face

Le nu provençal

(photograph by Willy Ronis, 1949)

The wooden shutter hanging open,
sunlight commands the shapes around the room.
A jug has left its ovals on a flagstone,
and tilts a little as if listening in
to a kneecap or a buttock.
                        Not so the chair
with one leg out of touch with everything,
about six feet away across the floor.

If a round mat covers several flagstones,
what of the swirl of shadows all around,
tipping the chair, invading the towel that hangs
from the rail of an iron washstand, burrowing
into the armpit poised above the bowl.

The bowl is luminous enamel and contains
two hands, from one of which an arm sprouts
rounding into the gleam across a shoulder.
The mat, woven of rushes, also supports
the lines of feet mounting past the ankles
into calves that curve up into little pits
of light back of the knees.

                        Above the bowl
a mirror on a string, and where the frame
swooshes down to complete another oval,
a smudge of hair, a flit of shoulder show.

And the hair itself is tucked against a nape
never to be seen because the back's ellipse
conceals it, with a ripple of its flesh
and muscles held in tightly to the backbone.

Least mysterious of all a nipple charms
the bowl of white light with its bud, which echoes
across delicate dark waves of flesh
                            and is there again
in the round bottom and its dusky cleft.

Watch as you will, the mystery is elsewhere.
Perhaps between the things, distributing tensions.
Perhaps in the diagonals which cross, from chair
to shutter through the body, from the mirror
downward across the body to the jug.
Or in the volume of the space they occupy,
for such a little time sifting the silence,
buttressed at one end by the puckered wall
of stone and plaster, at the other end
by the gaze exploring all without distress.

Third Generation

For two old immigrants
who do not speak the language
I drag this wooden dog
over the bending floor
of a corridor in their attic

It circles the town and crosses it
from one end to the other
many doors are swinging
open and shut as I pass
and the dog behind me clicketyclack

They lent me their plank
and played me the Mass in B minor
I lost the plank in a park somehow
or it turned into this dog
I am dragging for ever and ever

Old Woman at the County Dump

Sitting in her cracked hutch,
beneath trees, hidden from the road,
she is the guardian of a torrent
of burst mattresses, rust and rubber,
bodiless lids of objects without present function.

One tooth and a hank of hair,
a form of speech that spits and babbles
like the nerves of a scorpion in a jam jar.

Junk, mounds of it, from dark hollows
little dogs erupt, sniffing, stretch and disappear
like stars that fall in August. All the stuff
people have left, beyond and behind,
marching toward a world of absolute deodorants,
infallible laxatives.

               What if she died?
Who'd notice? She might be found,
a few ribs and shanks, hardly smelling at all,
at home among the vacant basins. Her apocalypse
the O all these unbolted toilet lids
trumpet to the skies.

At night, I imagine
stuck to her rocking chair, she dreams,
dreams of being guarded by the garbage.
A block of rusty bedsprings at her door,
plucked by rat claws, gives off
intermittent echoes of an old serenade.
With all its worms a portly wardrobe,
her protector.

I think of the lightning,
if it was lightning lashed from the waters,
the hiss of it, a sort of red
veined quaking cream, and frothed ashore
the whiff, a first, of space and time.

And I think of the women who floated
out of the forests, hard on the tracks of vague men,
thud of their feet, the wind's cry,
tall savannah grasses bending:
Some carry in hollow logs
a yellow flame.

Puffs of smoke
struggle up from her heap of clapboard.
Still she is the guardian
of an element that signifies
a good roast crackling, a legend to live by,
of power tamed and change.

History
has beaten most of the life out of her body,
but still the days flash on,
nights blossom with new moons, the people
burst through time, breaking things like toys,
and leave her the rubble.

The Fossil Fish
15 Micropoems

(Vaucluse: July-September 1969)

1

village quote idiot unquote
look a walking often takes
long at you

    stops & slow hows
    he come through

        screwy? clutched in
his one scrotum hand the other
crumpled hugs a fingering book

               2

          them squads in
       helmets
        burning
         the dragonfly's eyeballs
      out
     is just ants

    3

   & silver eggs on stems
     be nobbut topknots
of a grass – ah savage head
    see them caught
       nodding in the wind launch your airy
hundredfold
   parabolas of seeing

4

ivy around the capstone
starts to fizz:
early snailhorns are
sounding the systems
of their space

5

shorts white
at the sharp angle of
trim bronze legs
to a melon balanced
in one palm she subtends her
equilateral nose
deepening the hidden
rose of that sphere
between cone & cone

6

rock & bough
tumbled over slammed against
pluck out their fillets
of necessary flesh
mad pleasure
for once to bleed
on a hill groaning
with apricot trees

7

inside the shell, fields:
　　　　listen, lavender, wheat
behind it, blue
　　　　　　mountain behind
the wheat, the sun
over the mountain, curving
up, the wave murmur: it
　　　won't fall

8

storing its times
the body
learns weightlessness

space be skin
limit
my flesh of lightning

9

toad
crawls
up
boulders
always
dragging
his
ughs!

10

a place ribbed with quartz between
soaring
rock wings here the wind
swivels crashing sucked
back into its helix
luminous flesh in which
embedded far below beyond
float mountains little
mossy tuffets

11

feeling the leaf
a tree
wrote
spine
longwise it is not
chinese but crinkles

12

calm in the face of nature

.

fearful in the face of nature

.

maggot, neither, holes
up in a peach

13

to please a nymph
　　sip at her spring
so her true voice told
　　first a far cry
now sharper breaths
　　moisten this rosy moss
& soon for sure
　　she will be coming

14

coming also his long gusts tell me
the wind a river he roars
　　　in pine trees pounding walls of rock
to destroy he scatters to build

speech a silver breath & seed once he scooped
　　a whole man from a cave
　　　flicked him away
like an eyeball

　　　with twisted clay
trumpets at dawn we call for him hopeless
　　on the mountain

he floats in the crested ocean eastward
　　blue cattle waiting to drink
the first torrent of rays

　　how else from his flowering
chiselled hollows
　　could these bee snouts tap our honey

15

the fossil fish
hides in time
for now it is the season

& all the hunters come
with long clean rifles

Mérindol Interior 1970

Sheets of paper you wrap around me
Crucify me with a length of string
Tip me into the box and hopefully
I'm off by air to another place

There if it's blue the roof shores this ocean up
And a limestone kitchen hangs under our bed
My tappity spoon threads our bowls into a china harp
A glass of blood you stroke from the sobbing bottle

But we are branches now and I am thorned
For joy we prance in a whirlwind of quilts
Finches hopping from breath to breath we fatten
With kisses and nipples and cool cherries

Afterward your brown legs are not paper any more
I shriek for air entombed not in string
But in the furrows I have gouged all over you
My knife is tender truly it is a lamp you hold

Or in your town the houses are little orbs
With leaves eager to sprout and harsh beaks pecking
They circle the elms we sit beneath at night
Listening to drums beaten by maggots

Never can we reach a darker place than this
My hot oils drip on your belly and make us laugh
Again out of your looking glass I have come to you
Marked sender unknown return to addressee

The bringer of news has rushed through the gate
Without even the horror of a knock
He shows us the crop impaled on our prongs today
Naked children racing a sunburst of petrol

You wear the smile a lamb at pasture lives through
I touch the earth and regret my fingers
Several times I told you never to turn your head
The bull roars in his cave the mouse in his pit of smells

Brightness thickens the names
Old fountains clogging and the rain harsh
Darkens all that is done for us – on crusts of blood
Torn from the back of the world we spread our butter

On Mozart's Birthday

for Tom Raworth

Suppose a birth
& it is clarity
but what are the odds

or the way sudden words
of yours launch into a pure
unemotional space

now & here & by name
even these tasks
a referential bodymass

turned satellite
the Great Udder in orbit
fans through networks

trade cycles flashpoint
battle fronts
but few words from the quick

fleeting objectives
bring home
a faraway

figuration of earthglow
uncoop for some
the joy in a thing

altogether sexual
a high speed submicroscopic
impetus

& ever up against
that wall
before the blood be dry

gunners our lepidopterists
before they pin us down
we hear the wave

throb of Osip's
carbolic guitar
& clean through it

go the words go naked
steady torchbearers
to serve the wise unborn

first a spirit
listening for the ancestors
& then a rose

A Drive in the Country: Henri Toulouse-Lautrec

Drawn out of the bones of light,
Definite figures, a few, ordinary.

As if in its bones the light has known them,
All: the horse, trotting away,
The yellow trap, and in their Sunday hats
Face to face, the man and the woman.

Properly, half a man and half a woman.
Come to that, only half a horse.
Locomotion, yet essential muscles
Are hidden in the picture; even the dog,

Athwart, running behind the yellow trap
Like the wind – not a leg in sight.

Gone any moment,
Beautiful creaking old trap drawn by half a horse.
No, not that. It is the way
A definite hat plume centres everything
On a still point in the sky.

Or the hatcrowns compose
One imaginary diagonal streaking off
Into the sky's oblong blue; and it is nice,
The way it slants against the lower
Green diagonal of the field's edge.

Not even that. The dog – great cool gush
Of the air across his nostrils. Not that:
Shot with rose, an undulation of shadow
Racing the trap, a feather's cusp,
Magnified, as dog, and sideleaping
Not from a hat but from the road.

Not so, not so; a presence, tacit,
Holds in place, for the eye to strike them,
Fugitive signs in their consortium: an egg!

Interior oval, its yolk,
A yellow trap, the crystal sun chariot –
Across the emerald cone, an egg, tilted,
That is what the figures make and are made of.

Parabola, it begins
At the tip of the horse's ears, it hugs
The hatcrowns, rounds the dog's tail,
Returns to base along the curve from wheel to hoof.

Even then, not so.
It never was an egg. If not, what else,
What else but the eye of Henri Toulouse-Lautrec:

And hiding it had spied
Upon itself, slicing itself
In half, had scooped up this other universe
Out of the escaping bloody mucus; now
The figures dwelling in it,

Healed, flawless, are the very nerve
That sees, and they retreat from you
Because of this,
When all the time it happens to be there.

Anasphere: le torse antique

kami naraba
yurara-sarara-to
ori-tamae!

I

Among the grains how small you were
Dry in the desert of your image

You did not hear the cries of love as you passed
Down the street, you did not see
The spittle
Fly nor the beads of blood on the axe blade

The naked masked woman
Twice she swung it & once more & high
By its long handle

II

Here we are travelling from place to place

Here I keep you hidden
Held by a great lightness
Body & voice if I could set you free

In my cage a castle rose to its turrets
Only for mice & a flock of ravens
Pure columns unbent by thought

Here shall they flower from our stillness
Voice their future dream
Of being trees

Plant them giving shade in a field
For five cows composing a sign for us
The diagonals of a dice
Or it is the pentagram –
Hidden in a bed the conversation of bodies
Hidden I keep them

And still there is a voice
Whenever in sweet nakedness you nuzzle me
Voice I want you not only to say

A white cow is made of cream & fury

– Hathor

So your face took shape
It was in the boulders uphill before us
A movement of lines to the measure of a dance
A flashing of earth years Egyptian axes and eyes
No time at all in which it happens

One hundred thousand horses
Toppling off the crag were chopped into food
For the hands that peeled leaves of laurel
Out of the flint core
Now in a field of old rain goofily like a fortress
A red horse was planting his hooves
 – Look how it is to stand there

Devastation
Marks no tracks of ours
Lightly now through these hidden places we shall walk
Where mouths collect & change to make expressions
Listen
A street with many twistings this one

Lightly you are here you had no weight whatever
Wearing your little cloak over so much nakedness
You leaned against me

III

1

Body of light
    Dwelling in a piss jet
Or particular cherry blossom

Look, a spirit
Wanted something
A sign, to be manifest
In all directions

Never
Sure, inhaling itself
A whirlwind

2

Desire, pressing
On silence
To lure you, poem
One or two words

Go
To the southern shore
One flesh we pursue

3

One, through Never –
A span, slightest across
Perdition, horrible
Deep, the gurgle

It is
Pepper behind my eyes, it fashions
The eye of the hurricane
It fills
With snakes & stars
The liquid cathedral collapsing across
Atolls, Florida keys

4

World, great harp
Built of blood
Now then
What sounds in flight

What muscular forms of breath
Never flow, leap
Up the torrent & restore

To you
Your open tunes

5

One flesh –
Other, another
Horizon, ancient
Unplaceable

Twitter your speech again
Models
Out of oblivion
The bud & the wave & the snowflake

6

Your never is yes,
Out of nowhere the cry
Gone & again
Cupola, welling, spiral, it lifts from

The bird throat

Soon hushed

7

But song in
Some few broken
    Tombs

A touched sex

IV

Difficult
    Piecing the life together

        'like a supper in the wind'
How it comes, goes
            Exact from perception
Rhythm

            Not snatching
        It comes in waves
Not knowing me from you
    A spirit cannot be spoken
Or spoken of

Drums drumming the exact measure
Dancer to dancer the flower spray is passed

To build for you a space
          In this drain of being it is I
          Smash the heads & fix famine
A floor strewn with rock-orchid
                    Lotus roof

In mid-air, air dangerous with heat
               Carbonic gas, beams of cassia
I have suspended
          A floorspread weighted down with white jades

Margins, like these
          Then at sun up to have leapt into
The blue fragrant living sea

Profit motive melts the poles
                    Paris drowning, Bombay
Alexandria

I have hung strips of flesh at porch & gate
          The flesh of children

The time will not come again
                    It will not come again

[Note: the epigraph, from the twelfth-century Japanese text
Ryojin Hissho, means: 'If you are a god, / With a swing and a
swish/Deign to come down.' See Arthur Waley, *The Nine
Songs* (London 1955, p. 14), source for certain ancient
Chinese shamanic motifs in sections III and IV.]

In the Secret House

for Ann

Why lean over the fire, and who is this
Being
Vaguely human, who
Watches the steam float from wet boots
And regards the rose interiors

Various woods keep
Recomposing themselves; nothing holds
In the fire, the fire is always
Less than it was, the fire –

Expulsion
Of old smells, new intangible horizons
Does not hear through its decay,
Calling in the cold
Rain, the little owl, one note
Over and over

Nor, under its breath, does the fire give
A thought to the petrified
Print of a snail, its broken wheel –
Rays on a rock at the hearth's edge. Who
Is this, and who thinks

Through the fire, sees the rayed shell,
Solid axis, the whirling death
Of some incorrigible small thing
Before the ice came

Before the ice came carving out the mountain
And the fire took
Or took care of someone
And the house was constructed
In a cloud of goats, coming, going,
Before the cockerels

Put down their tracks, cry and claw,
Through generations, this fly
Settled on the breadloaf –

So stare, into the fire, and what for
The important
Citadel, towers of light, crepuscular
Tunnels, simply face
The black rain, blue wave
Of mountain birdsong

Mud on my hands, little owl, it is
No grief to share with you,
Little owl,
The one note, not lost, for nothing

Celeste

looks like them elementals just poured
a glass of blue champagne
and you look up
– silver fizz –
because your body
is
the stem

Discourse on Legend

I hug to my breast
The green head of wheat
And I suckle it
    Forough Farrokhzad

Legend, you are the one, the who
The woman jumping out of the global box
The song the wave the blue in the veins
Which has no completion

Try as I may to decipher you
I find no text at all;
When I riffle the book to find a rule
You escape, happily
Cleaning your teeth with a carrot;
Or a certain African king, for him
As you knot your hair and strip,
I hear you cough, ahem, in a vast
Green Sahara of hope and desire

Or you have cut the world's
Irascible droning
Throat and wallow, legend, you,
In the blood. You give yourself
To the hilt, yet
Every drop,
Your own undulant
Body drinks it back, freely the torrent
Returns, and you, legend,
Swing through the maze with never a blank
Drawn, from pulse to pulse. Speak

And you rip heads off
The cardboard
Categorizing men who try
To read you. Laugh

And you speak a song, I hear it
Far off as the wind
Sucks and guzzles
A single grain of sand and whips
The flesh of moons
Wicked habit tramples. Legend,

Do not be deceived
By the mechanical gesture,
Yours or any. Do not think
That you repeat yourself
To death.
You'll die more easily, with a croak
In a goatskin tent, in Italy a cough,
A flash of your laugh
May extinguish you
On a ship, but not this, not

You, anonymous,
Crosseyed
Kissing your knee, not
For fascination fingering your bush
All curled up in a madhouse.

But
But I could be wrong
I could be wrong, and when or where
It starts, the track of this
Incomprehension, I alone (this
I whom you
Provoked and

Must ignore) can ask. Of what? *Ecoute*,
O godforsaken oracle, *écoute* . . .

If it is in
A certain falsity, which bends all sense
When thought like twilight
Spirals up from its depth to meet
A promise of connection, legend, is it you

Multiplies and snarls the track,
Do all the flying
Jagged particles
Connect
By grafts drawn from the dark
Body of legend?

You, distinct, and
No other, but
Escaping
Autodestruct, so
Like a civilization bent on death
You might be a messenger, come
From the core of life with his tongue cut out,
Or a mirror
In the pure
Instant as it falls
To the stone floor, and

From the impact, shattering, has
Already arisen the wand of mimosa,
Yellow, without
Fracture, stillness in a room,
A melon is glad to be round like that,
Lips parting, listen, the first
Sound
Of a speech for an exchange

Of natures
Between things and people, a joy arises also
Giving this blue to the sea,
To the city its dawns and sacred statues

And in some, legend, among us
A spirit responds, not
So as to speak of it, with a longing
To be
Reborn.

Caromb, Vaucluse

For the giant boy who plays
Alone
Pétanque in a yard

For the idiot girl
Who sings at the wrong time
Stone feet
Plunged in a dance of fish

For the white & yelping
Imbecile afloat
In the same old stream

Listen to the shriek
It is only the hirondelle

This rush of wings

Listen to the fly, it is not a fly
The buzz of weight
Is fattening a fig

Which you peel, as is right
They say
Never peel a peach
You need not fear

This blue tint on a vine leaf
The shivering part
Of sunrise

Snail on the Doorstep

Snail on the doorstep
Is it rain or dusk
Plants giving off odour of sheep's fleece
So strong the curls cling
Wet between fingers

Snail on a doorstep far south
A radio knob you want to turn it
(Knees crack as you crouch to see it)
For news and think another catastrophe
News counts the decay
And substance of sacred things

Snail on the doorstep knees cracking
Light from nowhere
Point like a pyramid strikes the shell
Strikes the ultimate
Spiral centre

It is this expanse only an expanding
Centre of the spiral
The light stops where it started
But the snail on the doorstep
Uncoils in the light and blooms

The pyramid whispering expands
It follows the infinite curve of space
It ends where it started
If this were not a snail
There could be no universe

If this were not a snail
Another door would not let out

These children
They would not have crept
Under the mulberry on tiptoe
Fingers to their lips

All the snails would roll
Hightailing it away from them
Startled horns aswish to test
Cooler air
Not spirals like the sun

Hearing Elgar Again

for D.M.M. at 75

Not crocked exactly, but in a doze,
There I was, before supper time: Elgar,
Stop your meteoric noise, the glory
Leaves me cold; then it was
I woke to the melody –

Back, a place, 1939, and people
Singing, little me among them,
Fresh from a holiday
Summer, beside the Cornish sea, I sang
In chorus with a hundred English people.

You choose to live, as far as possible,
Spontaneously. So life is all
A wandering – curious orchestra, the whole
Sound of it accords with such
Invention of melody, song half-buried

By tympani, trombones, the glorious hot
Imperium. A life proceeds,
It is all, all of it, found in the instant:
Look, flowing, a friend shone, but wizards,
Drunken, forgot what I have to say

And underneath, in her garlic subway,
Busbied Persephone stands and waves
Her tambourine, a rabbit
Drums little feet on a village green, the snare
A moon halo strangling him.

Mother – we have gone on while others,
We remember, flew as ash into the sky.
To what? We have gone
On, dense trees, birdsong in cool petals
Never the ignored sustenance;

Rolling music is what deceives us, only
An appetite springs from the core, –
Melody, in a flash,
A harsh frog croaks in the creek now,
A bit of rain has touched my hand. Why?

How to Listen to Birds

Put no trust in loud sounds
Learn from the crystal
Ladderings of music

To listen: bodily. Slip
Through the rifts which model
Their notes. A moment, one, day
Or night, may be a more favoured
Time

For penetration: one tiny spool
Of the unseen
Unrolls from a chirrup. Feel

Feel again its formal flute alarm,
The wave creation –
A dancing woman's hair, it floats
Across your face –

A note or two, at last,
Concentrates the practised world
Into some new thing;

Wake, otherwise, attentive
To such a call, you might
Inhale the first perfume on earth,

Touch the ghost,
Voluminous, of a howl tight coiled
In the plain tune,

Or find no way of your own
To speak
Belief, at a variance so fine
It modifies the whole

Machine of being: this
Is not unpolitical.

The World First

Emptiness, the emptiness in you
Fill it, fill it with, I don't know,
Something, not with toys, not with

Mythologies, fill it
With something, no, you can't, with solid
Villages, or seas, bottle corks, desire,

Inconspicuous bent nails, almost anything,
Fury of enemies, whatever grips
Fill the emptiness for fear

Fill it for never ending
Fill the emptiness or it will tear off heads,
The heads you love, watch them, down the drain

Float like yours, the heads,
Howl and tumble, torn off, not much
Not much to hold on to

Fill the emptiness, facing it, raw grief
Now and really surrounds your face,
Fill it with that, if you can, the world first

And do not dwell on it, laborious, only,
Shapeless hole, seize it, can you,
Scattered curse, you can't blot it out

But clear figures, more than imagine
Other worlds, they spin with other feeling, fill it
Fill it with them, you can't, trackless

No map, impenetrable, specific, you
Can't, but make them dance it out, different,
Muscular and trim, repeat it over and over

Only to yourself, can you now, the emptiness,
Know it inside out, always there,
The great sucking emptiness you keep

Replenishing with towns, the birds, a river,
Roofs of old tiles red and wet with dawn,
You can't, it is always there, control

Impermanent in the timed flight of words;
And with your interior animals refresh it,
In first light they do face one another, free

Not spellbound, not,
By the gaze of any remote Upholder,
When for them you invent an open deep indwelling,

Can you, and a secret air, for there you plant
Under the clocks and mouths, under the drums
No foundation without fault, emptiness

Not like this, a turning around, but to be made
Into the holy field of apple trees
If death itself be no more strange or final.

History of Not Quite Everything

Slamming of a car door outside
Is it you
A burst of music like sea waves human feelings
Turn over and over
Is it you the silvery heat of thigh to thigh

Because my jalopy was radioactive
They took me to the nut house for testing
The hooded lunatics happy as sandboys
Did their dance in a ring

Was it you
Beside me the air with your shape in it
Rustling was it you Hungarian girl with twelve grenades
Went under the tank and blew it to pieces

Between our bodies nothing but the moon stood
Nothing was ever wasted
There was time enough twelve years but was it you
Before I died under a tree we had fallen asleep
Was it you woke up and screamed for a hundred years

And forgotten words who spoke them
Head of a halibut who cut it off
A driftwood stick in sand
Who rammed it into the fish throat from under

Or the provision of justice under law
Is it you
Drenched in blood these were hungry babies
Old men froze by the roadside
Is it you very gentle fingers on the long march

Is it you very gentle fingers
Silent void
The voice
I must go on answering for ever

Ibeji

African figurine on a desk
This morning,
Polished with lemon oil, hoists
More high his furrowed hairdo,
Deepens his frown

Abstraction pulls from him a living
Crystal shape, distinct
From books he blinks at; dark wood
Sprang from a tuck in time, but lord
What loops one lives in –

Day's action crushes
The mulberry, then drink at seven,
With one kick bourbon the flamingo
Restores to its native
Air the toothless pink soul

Funny for once it looks, the pit
Of delusion. You wonder at
The skill: what intuition gouged
Three angled dents in his forehead, silver,
Even the tilt of his mouth

Cheek scars plummet to the corners
To force a smile. A nail gores
One eyeball. A sneeze
Might anytime explode. The belly
A column of root – it has returned

His ancient feel for trees
To the whittled beast, worm-eaten
Man. And it is good
When the door creaks open, to find him in
Still, only him.

Wild Horse

As a more or less literate person
Who writes down things that have
Some connection with the English language

What should I do with a wild horse
Suddenly presenting itself to my thoughts
In Berlin this winter morning

Under no circumstances would I write
About a wild horse in a manner approaching
That of the savage Mr Ted Hughes

I cannot recall that I have ever
Seen a wild horse in the flesh
Perhaps in films but I have not smelled one

Not once even from afar I have not
Watched a wild horse glow in the moonlight
I have never touched one who has?

I do not live in Marlboro Country
I have no spurs no saddle no skill
I cannot even ride a tame horse but this one

This wild horse has given me a shake
Bucking inside me   One moment it is
Chestnut brown like a cello

The next black as Pelikan ink
And white the next like nothing
On earth   Pitiful comparisons

The thing is all muscle and fury
It is controlled as a star is said to be
By certain magnetic conditions

The thing is abrupt   It hears
Who knows what and is off like the wind
In pursuit or going just anywhere

It stops to drink from a pool
Hoofing it over a hill   cropping
Prairie grass   Impulse grips it

This horse but in that grip it is free
Knowing in its bones a radiance
Which I ride like a speck of dust

Bareback   Can the reason be this belt
I bought from a junkstore north of La Grange
Texas?   Its oval buckle with a horse

Embossed on it was first prize once for riding
Bareback in a rodeo   Influences must have
Penetrated my guts gone to my head

Or does it just come at a gallop
This wild horse because a few friends
And loves these past few months have

Irradiated my body with something keen
Intrinsic to the universe a power
I would not dream of questioning

Or putting my name to   Don't look down
Or behind   Fly in the fury of the horse
With wild love   They'll drag you off

Soon enough ordinary humdrum things
Is what I tell myself feeling it
And I'm up there all right this very moment

Thinking of you Ann Alberto Caroline
And you Tsëpë Romanian clown my friend
And someone else I'll put no name to

I'm up there all right the world's force
Hits me bends back my spine but hell
Head up I'm going through the crosswinds

Clean with the perfume of Saint Elizabeth's Weed
Or what is it called over the hills and down
Uhlandstrasse   If this is a lion I say hallo

Raccoons fling me nuts which I catch
Reaching a hand up as I pass beneath
Cheerful pecans the looped vines the sweet

Sophora   Sun shines all day   Is this
An exaggeration? Probably it is
But this wild horse under me knows best

How to crash through hope the barrier
Shielding the helpless
And how best to help this blaze the universe

Propel itself by subtle shifts
And twistings of the shoulderblades
Onwards   Deep orange canyons then scrub

Flats tender tamarisk cactus flowers whizz
Drumming   Its hooves are my heartbeats
Mine its flying sweat silken tail floats out

Into spaces which contract behind us
Bleeding shadows across the kicked dust
At moonrise   To the tinkle of waters

We listen listen the great crag blossoms
Indigo with a hundred faces cut by the ray
From horn and cleft   We watch watch

He appears the magician with his finger
Beckoning the sharp interior form unfolds
Across rock mass   Profile gaze upstream

To where the waters
We now stoop to drink
Have come from

Old Water Jar

Like one of the old ideas
It won't hold water any more
But it is round in the belly
And has strong bladed
Shoulders like a good woman
Elegant even the curves
Run down from the mouth
In a long sweet wave
You can't help liking it so
Simply for the way
It stands there

Jacob's Hat

The great boled oaks lift up their limbs
To paint the air

But Jacob's water bottle and his cloak
Are heaped beneath his hat

And the sheep and the shepherd on horseback
Have somewhere else to go

Is it not curious, Jacob's hat?
The crown is tall, of straw, the broad brim

Crumpled like the edge of a mushroom,
No, the top lip of a madman

Take your eye off it if you can
To watch Jacob's knee

Ram the groin of the angel or gather
The muscle tension

Making a shadowy ocean of
The flesh on his back

You do not hear the sheep bleat
Or the river ripple

You do not choke on the dust kicked up
By the shepherd's horse

You might not even notice the painting oaks
Or the spear laid across

Jacob's bundle of belongings, or the sword
Dropped in its sheath

Only the hat absorbs the shock of attention
An old straw hat

For all the world like a skull fungus
Doffed evidently by Jacob

Who took time enough to put in order
His precious few belongings

And with his well worn hat crown the heap
Before he sprang at the angel

In Anatolia

Slit eye, so young, in your place,
I mean no harm, but see you
And am close, in this light, so
Close. Food, knives, a red floor peak
And are gone in your flesh glow. The curve
Of a bird comes back to me.

Yes, it was big, as birds go. Blue wings,
A throat, I think, rain-rose, and a crest.
All at once it flew out of no place.
It perched on a plinth of white stone
To flute the one song it knew.

Noon: heat in this old town spent
Long breaths on rock. Wells dry. A few
Cubes of shade. Candid weeds made sure
The song could last. Pure notes
Go well with dust; in the doom of that high place
Time showed its drift.

On that plinth it put down claws, a bird,
Spikes – it told the air
What it meant: *io dio*, it sang. *Io dio*.
You will not say it. Your hair is
Coiffed to fall, soft, across your face,
As if your face should not be shown here –

A wing, gloss, when
You shake your head like that you hide
Most, at least, of your face. Wax
Boys, they sit, one by one, dumb, with hands
They fold and twist, here, at this feast:
You do not foot their bill.

Rich you might be, or
Not, but are you here? Your place seems
Close to oak boards, wild rice, raw fish.
That blue bird, you are with it.
Still you have ways to resist
Dead mouths, our small norms, blood that froze,

So much heart ache. Why, white stones
Once were grooved, to hold up roofs. White
Stone, fierce hands hewed it
Into forms. Through the fresh
Stone robes a god flew, those days, a pulse
It was thought. Worse off by far,
We have none or put ours in the wrong place.

Stand there and speak. Tell
Why no springs flow there. Why no folks walk
The old streets. Did the no-good bird
Eat the gods up? Let your wing fall
To hide your face. We do not know
What now to fear most.

Pink Slippers

Pink slippers –
The voices
Return, the voices
From Antioch, Agrigentum, wherever
Return, clear

Splitting apart
The bottled, rotten
Remnant we
Dwell in, with a swish
Of clothes falling

From limbs radiant
The voices
Return. She stood
And shook
Off everything, stood

In the silver light
A moment,
In a forest, in
A city, ancient lamps
Marble paving –

And the pink
Slippers? Later they
Crossed
A road, other feet
Than hers in them,

But to death
He loved them. Pink
And voices, distinctly
They spoke, delivering the drift
Of old stories –

Wickedly
The swish, the dark
And silver joy, the arms
Holding, the perfect
Fit, immediate

Relic

Powdered wood from a beam
And plaster from the ceiling
Sift into dunes among the random
Worm-holes peppering my desk.

Overhead the flying machines
Buzz, on their occasions. I admire
The hood worn by the lime tree;
Scent of its flowers, I breathe it in.

They cluster in threes or fours, like bells;
Bees in the hood and scarabs hum;
The bird with a black mask stops to listen,
Spidery claw on a flagstone.

I am wondering at the fluency of its lines,
And how the tail flits, when all at once,
At the top of the winding stair,
You stand in a torrent of light,

Dressed in silver linen, as you wave,
Hatless, ready to go, your sleeve
Uncaptured, a spray of flower bells
Tilting across the tassel of your parasol.

A Road that is One in Many

for George and Mary Oppen

This is a little road, this part of it
Like the centre bar of an old hand drill
Runs straight from this bend to the next

Hold tight when you walk along it
Violet orbs revolve under the pebbles,
Daily shadows. These vines have grapes

Shrub vines, bitter grapes, mustang. Hold tight
When this bird spider hauls his thick ass
Over the tarmac, this pothole is his

Hold tight to your straight walk, tiptoe
Certain spots are swept by heat
That is what blows, that is what dries

The inside of your mouth. The signs
Droop or rust, are not adequate
To the events they warn about. Warn

The pecan comes late into leaf, the big
Pecan; that is juniper, a cone, house
Of a singing bird. The signs do not sing

Being, but collisions, they take sometimes
A life or two. Hold tight, don't roll off, all
Sorts of people have walked along this road

The road is old, new, was Indian trail
By water, TU, they said, water; now
Corvettes and subarus, few foot people

This field in summer clings to a thatch
Of slow dragonflies; now nothing lives
In the tin shed, or is it nothing, only

Bugs, but you can moo to the ghosts
Of seven extinct preoccupying cows. Not
A slope in sight. These black

Eyed susans are the prettiest flower,
Later the dayflower marks its own distinct
Fluting off against this sky of skies

And the white rain, the white rain lilies
Really are these fragrant acid fruits
Of rain. Soon it stops. Under the polestar

At night hold tight still, grip this
Ground with your unshackled feet,
Don't scare these vines or ghosts are

Vines and ghosts. At night the lake
Is good for a swim. Don't mind these bats
That flit crisscross close to the cooling

Surface. Hold tight just once again,
Then let go and be consumed by the cool.
This is in the things and shines in the things.

An Old Wine Press

1

An old wine press
With its iron screw
Column down the middle –
Vertical slats doubly hooped
Contain the tub – this instrument
Sepia on account of its being
Not the very thing but a photo dated
No later than 1910

2

Higher up, steep slant of a barn roof.
The line of its eave like a lip,
Wavy. A sort of monster
Grin goofily reveals
The stubs of seven teeth, unless
These are beam ends or swallows' nests

3

And halfway up the slant
Two holes are built, like little eyes, or else
They breathe for the hayloft, handy
Homes of dove, dark lodges
For the grape-scented air

4

All this no more than a glimpse
But the barn behind the wine press caught
And carries onward
A human imprint, rough hewn
A flicker of the torch

5

Here for once
Doubly precious, considering these
Eight people grouped around the press:

Just a bunch of farm folk, three generations,
The men clothed in stained denims, sweaty caps;
The woman has pinned a flower to her breast
And holds an empty cheese basket;
A little boy has curled his fingers
Around the handle of a hooped
Wooden wine jug

There they stood, tilting
Every which way; splay feet, beefy arms
Dovetailed into a right good
Angular design:

Three men
Lean against the tub on its platform;
If this beard might crumple into a king's mask,
Still clog and boot crack with mud
And glue these

Dancers to the ground; the boy
Hangs in the middle, perched, dangling
Tiny booted feet –

Any moment
The glass he grips by the stem will spill;
Oddly tender yet, the way
All around him thicker fingers hold
The scarce seen cool substance –
In it gleams the god, red and savage,
Spinning the world for more than money

7

Yet the money matters. You can plot
Grim pursuit of it in the skew
Cheek folds of the white-haired man.
Hope made the woman's mouth
A thin long line and in her round chin
Totted up
Credits of hair, winnings of eye, decimals
Of nostril

Who knows, it is mostly too late;
The wine that time at least
Had a fair chance;
The footwear might see another ten years out,
As good as a second skin, these denims
Are worn as the sun
Wears its light, or as the god they nourish
Squid-wickedly has thrown
History over his tentacles, a robe
Smoky in colour, a tissue of bloodstains,
Whose, fading, sepia

.

After a Noise in the Street

It is the small
Distinct image, old as you like,
On a coin, or silvery
In a daguerrotype

Speaks to me:
The trooper Probus,
Two centimetres high, at most,
Helmeted, sloping

A spear
Across a shoulder,
Condenses all
The gas of empire

Into a few
Quick signs. No fuss, either,
Had perplexed her face,
This young and tawny

Woman, but
An anger, fine, makes
Luminous now the eyes
She levelled in Nebraska

At the lens, never
Exhausting it, for the hands
Folded and slender in her lap
Siphon a torrent

Of feeling through the image.
There is anguish
Untrapped, an ardent
Breath sets free to fall

A dew as on a cherry,
To magnify, by sharpening
So far, the resolute
Infinitesimal flesh, this wisp

Of being, only this
A mortal
Tentatively manifests. A
Measure just

One fraction grander could
Put back
Into the spear
Slaughter;

Distend a pleat
In this dress, or blow
A tassel up
Beyond belief – and it lumbers

Back into the flimflam;
An embossed cuirass,
Probus any bigger, snagged
In power's mesh

Spills, as a blur, or boast,
His contracted time
Into the heaving
Primordial pettiness.

Cabaret de la Canne, January 1855

Sir, I do not know your name,
Nor do you know mine. So we sit,
Briefly, at neighbouring tables, you
With your bottle, the cat on your knee,
I with my little glass.

In our sunken ship
The third table has been taken
By the fine man of darkness, whom
We do not see. Look, on the furrowed surface
Glittering still, the flake of snow I flicked
From the collar of my coat when I came in.

Each sits watching
The face of his own slowly turning
Universe. Particularly the cat
Has known how the heat
Comes and goes. Important smells
Wrinkle and flex into signatures, you know,
Writ small in snowflakes and the skeletons
Of leaves. Shuddering,
The fingers of a spirit ink into our skins
Mysterious names, numbers, and messages.

Ancient gutters
Accommodate the cat, providing
Fish, spare ribs, a scrap of lamplight;
Spilt milk to lap up, now and then.

There are places where people turn yellow,
Having nothing to eat. Cloacas, attics.
Broken roofs. Through holes the snow sifts.
A Valois song can be issuing, in another street,
From a little girl's lips
For a penny.

Mandolins, a lantern swaying, make it
Difficult to want less than a tree to dance with.
Do we suffer
Most because the bunched worms will hang
In the emptiness you are looking at, this
Dome of mine, bald, this bony cabin?
                              What is immortal
If not the injustice?

There was a room I lived in once,
I remember how the early light in it
Fell across two rescued Fragonards.
There was a girl, nearly naked she was,
Tigers ran before her on a leash
And a little donkey woke us, braying,
Or a barge trumpet's echo off the river.

Like a swift in his globe of crisp mud
I hung between sleep and waking
And heard the straw speak in my thin
Mattress. Look, here it is, another face
Of that same
Towering light, again
In this bit of a rainbow, at its peril
Afloat in eau-de-vie:
I drink it for the dream that spills
Into life.

They tore it down, it was an old house.
They did not tear down
The other room, which, if you follow me,
We put there, suspending it
Outside any space that iron balls
Can shatter.

In that room the last vine still grew,
A veiny green, very ancient.
The last vine, first planted when
The emperor was Julian and Paris Egypt.
From that vine,
Yes from it you might see
A light as from the original stars unfolded

And flew as it pleased, to vary
As it touched the featured walls through
Twelve emotions. With snaky lines
It marbled the stones and old chairs
We had broken by leaning back to laugh.
To eye the stones was to feel a flow
Of female warmths and hear the goddess, –
Moan and shriek of the sistron in her fingers.

What can you be thinking?
No, do not indispose the cat.

Rilke's Feet

1

Heart bowels hand head and O the breast
So many of the parts fan out
Pressing on speech
Each a shape distinct
At length delivered a message
Classified sensitive

2

Perched in my tree as the light
Tries to unfold over Wilmersdorf

Rilke's feet a phrase
Ran amok in the mass below –

But in the grass
Not a trace left – playing

Woodland god he walked there
Barefoot – before architecture

Boiled the green to stone gray –
1897: I had taken my shoes off . . .

3

Sweetheart, Lou

. . . what is God, Mama?

                    "White hinds
                hidden in a thorn thicket"

No compliment to the long
Undulant chevelure of Magdalen

On a billow of mud
                in the Dordogne or Ariège was it
A footmark printed
                lightly
Hard mud in a deep cave

Might last another 15,000 years

But Rilke's feet
                he left them
                                standing
To be invented

4

This hot pursuant of
The Incomparable

A sort of hassock stool
He kept and kneeling on

Upholstered velvet
Worshipped any woman

He had invited no
Not any but this

Was the way he tended
Kneeling on the stool

And gazing up as
She waved an arm or

Cringed and bit her lip
Footless for some quaint

Antiphallocratic reason he
Poised at hers

A projectile
In a catapult

5

Or Rilke had no feet at all
What he had was fins
Up he twiddles into the air

Sycamore seed going the wrong way
Lands in my tree
Owl's eyes large liquid

Blink at me   Contrariwise
He had no body just a head
Thought a little girl

No body in his clean but threadbare
Clothes crossed the room
And took a cake with Mama later

Off again
Somehow bowing
Where can he have put that cake?

6

More famous feet
Than these invisible ones
The foot of Philoctet-
Es and Byron's

Hoof with its iambic knock
On the deck of a gondola,
Incidentally – copper,
His horse adored the hot

Weight of it and ladies
Lifted fingers to their eyes,
Thrilling stomachs
Fancy the surprise

Suddenly milord is dead
While muttering Greek
Bandits around his bed
Frenetically seek

To screw the damn thing off,
Here's Philoctetes' foot
Festering in a cave –
His wound minute by minute

Throbs away the years,
Four thousand of them spin
Till Troy falls to hexameters
And Rilke's feet begin

7

A Wicked One
When he scraped the Many
Bits together
Must have made some funny faces

Rilke's feet – how
Is this body
To be looked upon: a

Screen or
Not sure a
Scene a recipient interim

And liminally
In and over it creation's
Wavering shapes break open
Yet

Are distorted it is
The dance but done
As if by hangmen

Touch and look
From a footsole run
Tightrope lines to every single organ

8

Voice where are you now
Tree what has become of you
Never a column or pedestal

But a tree of branching blood vessels
A tree trying to speak
Through thunderous pumping of juices
I climb across this voice
In the grip of its twig deletions

9

Hands whose touch is thinking
    How the taste of orange flows
To the beat of a ringdance

Slowly out of its givens
    The automatic body
Builds itself

Might balance feet with
    Strong straight
Articulations but dammit

An orchestra of echoes
    Code of interchanging
Trait and ancestor

All we can see in one photo
    Is Rilke in
Well shone shoes with spats

Its constant monologue
    Broken by torture
Reroutes no signals

And a shoe might hide
    One discord perhaps a hand
Froze an insurgent impulse

And clogs
    In the negative
I am told

Now like an undesired
Eyeball captive in a pod of skin
For fingers wished it

Footward as a pipesmoker
Tamps tobacco
Down to the base of the pipe bowl

So blue huggermugger knobs
    When bones obtrude strum on tendons
Fuming toes

Recoil to plot
    Inversion of the message
Train to be fingers and pluck back

Their slice of the power
    Did Rilke then support a claw
Brain-limb feedback

Did it flush his touch of sphinx
    Faintly at the tip
With repression's rose

10

Rilke's feet
Wading in a weird
Kettle of fish

    The lobster
Has gone for a walk
With his ghost
The sea
Once
Too often

11

Xenophon Xenophon it were fit to include
Dark as it is again in Wilmersdorf
An echo of your script from Corinth, your
Fictional grammar of the human foot

Anabasis uh I am tired and my secret
Reader wonders where we have got
As did your mob of Greeks thirty years before
Thirty years before you finally wrote

A bit boastfully about the march to the sea
Then how your lines inch by inch
Barrelled along the barbarous coast

But hardly anyone cares now
About the fleetfooted Carduchi
Peltists and bowmen coming up quick

When they shoot they put the left foot out
And rest the base of the bow on it
Drawing back the string

You must have stopped to see that

And soon backwards the snow
Is opening its white tomb

Illshod columns of infantry
Straggle into the Armenian mountains
Was there no shit they could not bite through

Newly flayed oxenskin
Froze that night to the footsoles
Thongs cut into ankle flesh

Many perished
Snowblind thwacking spear on shield
Throat racket body racket made the foe
Feel outnumbered

Small bags later we tied
To the horse hooves else
In the snow to their bellies they sank

Can I speak to you now Rilke
As we sleep
A little for our lives
Though I wonder sometimes what you meant
And my memory is awful
The footless motions you enact or track

In poems where the verbs
Amaze by their precision
Were you pointing
Beyond the combative body which engulfs
All as nothing with its bubble

Pointing to a body more like music
A luminous relator with its warmth
"Transfiguring the earth"
If it was this what have we got
Not evil quite wondrous desires
But injustice

It may be too late
Your invisible
Feet can do nothing but insist
Issue into a space all
Rondure and volume void

Of anything more dense
Than the thrum of air you felt
Around a seagull's wing
As it poured the pearliness in
And fitted feathers

Threadless motion
Through it your truant feet
Sprinkling punctures might
Sustain
Like intervals between them utterly

Determined throngs of stars
Or freely quickening and distinct
These feet it is
That ease
The gasps of joy from children's throats

A Pinwheel

In his luggage X had stowed a green
Bronze arrowhead. The thing
Came from Armenia, Persian, he said.
Successive satraps in its time
Had all the best Armenian horses herded
South to the Persian king,
Rugs, tubs of turpentine, oil in jars,
Boys tactfully picked –

        On the mantelpiece
Y had a stemmed
Wooden cup from Crete. A convict
Made it. You might think
Fingernails not a knife had oddly
Whittled its
Maze of facets, groping for the tilt
It had to stand at. Piss gold the colour
That man's privation wept
And sorrow sweated into it –

236

Since 1940, Z
Has kept a coin, Macedonian. Curly head
Of Zeus on one side. Philip II
Leans forward, if you turn it, on a high
Stepping horse. Silver tunic still
Flutters around his body.
Silver hat brim twisting in the wind –
Years to go before the drink got him
Or bugles blew, at crack of dawn, and Alexander
Floated off, unblinking, in a cloud of archers.

Hot Bamboo

My roots go
sideways
only
they
will
never
grope deep
nohow can
these
hollow
shafts
hold
remembrance
whenever
sounds
trickle
flute
gong
from
the crackpot's

pretend house
I
want you
moonlight
(if you
will)
to waft
them
over a touch
a merest whiff
will
send
me

responding
with a shiver
on my way
down
growing
to the hut
impossibly
a lake
is
there
an early
heron
suspended
in a mist
now
drinks
this
open
sky
limbs
of wild plum hide
old scrolled

                    mountain
                        so
                    spread
                     your
                      fan
                     soon
                    sighed
                    bamboo

A Different Banquo

for Alberto de Lacerda

A ghost speech
I bring you, with my voice.
When you have gone, my voice will be forgotten.

Ghost speech I
Said, friends. But it's not quite
So far along. Here we are, if still we are

Not yet dead,
Nor gaga. True, any
Moment, any, could for ever extinguish,

Think of it,
The wave. So I ask you:
Remember things I said for fun, not insult,

Even when
Your ears, I said – they're big,
Can you wag them? Or: your lisp kissed sawdust. That

Little mole
On the tip of your nose –
A beacon? Could it guide through storm a long ship?

Can you switch
It off? Does it send up
Punctual signals? Intrusive things like that

I said. In
Hope you'd be provoked. In
Fear a soul might then respond, giving me back

Tenfold the
Joy it was to be there,
Humbly, with you, facing you, in natural

Light. The crust
Of this planet under
Us. Or yawning through our reckless candle flames

The abyss,
Unaccountable. To
Your memory admit me and my weird jokes;

The help I
Ever was to you need
Be no further concern. Still, hold against me

Failings, or
Possibly pettiness
I showed at times when talk ran wild, was too grand

– When you die
I said, Lord, you'll say, back
I come now, but he'd never known you were gone –

For a voice
Can be wrenching, can pluck
Out of a sky the moon, full, mute, properly

Blent with it.
Yet will you raise me up
Again, at your feasts? Also in lonely rooms

Which exist?
Drink whole flasks of me, raw
Red wine, never negligent? Give me a chance.

As for what
I wrote – thumb through it on
Weekdays, and skip, if you will, the rotten bits.

Or else, by
And large, have done with it.
Save your breath to resist contenders, who kill;

Cruel pack
Rats, they are organized,
And horror has no end. Acquiescent, I

Cried out, but
The soul in that sound was
Gashed by evil's claw. Heart now full, vacant soon,

At the beck
And call, leastways of drab
Manipulators, don't we all bide our time?

Little mouse,
With your voice now I shriek,
So small I made myself, hoping to slip through

Power's mesh.
Not good enough. I had
Chosen to be trapped. To be free was far too much

Breath wasted.
So greed abolishes
Good things, and the canny have no place to go:

Thus we loved,
We did, wildly, trusting
One passion. For, divisible, we only

Loved one voice,
Soaring, not mine. It comes
From the sky, weeps, laughs, shakes into shape our trees.

Lento

To be almost unable to wake up
To see the shadow of a spider's web
To be interested in it sleepily

To notice that the shadow is active
To wonder about its reiterated movement
To think its movement varies from time to time

To call it ocean
To feel it living in the room
To lie full length in the golden light the room contains

To hear the clatter of plates in the courtyard
To forget the shadow of the spider's web
To open the door and approach the plates

To feel hunger
To recognize that your hunger is privileged
To raise your arms

To take a knife in one hand
To take in the other hand a fork
To consider the veins in the marble table top

To admire on your plate a grilled ocean
To eat a helping of spider pie
To taste the white infinitive wine

Rosenkavalier Express

Sundown in the dining car of the Rosenkavalier Express –
   I am seeing the packed trees and fields of wheat,
Dense greens involved with depths of indigo,
   For the sun – all day it shone like nobody's business,
And I think that a poem should be like these
   Packed trees and wheat, a tuft aglow, an indigo thing;
Then for a split instant I'm happy, a thrill goes through me,
   The dinner of beef and wine, shock of a salty
Taste in the beef, the red ordinary wine,
   Might account for it, but robuster than any reason,
Visceral or not, is the briskness of it, I mean
   The spasm, spliced with a sweet tinge of doubt
Whether I'd be up to voicing a poem like that.

And there was the whole day sunlit in Vienna,
Hungover a bit after hours of drink with friends;
    I am still out on a walk at one in the morning,
The big idea was to find, at last, the Mikado,
    But I couldn't, so now I'll never be sure
If a special whore called Josephine hangs out there.
    I am still strolling around at one in the morning
Though it is eight p.m. and as the train swings
    Westward into the night, fields will be warm as beds,
A peace envelops me from eyebrow to anklebone,
    I want to say thank you to someone for letting me
Eat and drink and feel on my flesh, whizzing by,
    These tufts of pine, these depths of indigo,
Rhombs of wheat that surge in the wind;

    Birds and rabbits will be rustling through them,
Smells drift, sprung by sun from June rain,
    Prickly smells of wing and fur, rose and lettuce,
Search in me for the tautest bowstring, holding
    But lightly holding the midpoint of the bow.
Ah well, the Mikado stroll was a washout,
    But with coffee there comes a little sugar packet
With "Mikado" printed on it, and a gasp, childish
    Enough – I catch my breath as the large
Rhythm of coincidence wraps me in a fold of fire.

    What is this? Moneyless but sometimes lucky
I have been ways with women that made them powderkegs.
    Wrong, time and again, I have wounded people,
Fallen short of their dreams, risen to them
    Too little or too late; less and less I can tell
What feeling is good for, but have been acquainted
    With animals fierce and beautiful, so to whom,
To what should I give thanks, and thanks for what?

244

What have I brought to love, if not catastrophe?
Now ideas flock like moonsheep in my turning head,
    Now I see roof angles, wooden cabins in cabbage plots,
Goalposts and staircases, and so rotund a hill,
    O, distance slips into its blue mist, but point blank
Stalks of wheat and blades of grass freshen again.
    As if through me Imagination wanted, sightless,
To fondle volumes of objects and read their legends,
    Trim old barns and now the Danube, full stretch,
Open lips that motion to speak, wag their tongues.

    So I think of the tongue of the blackbird,
And that I won't call this moody aria "Mitteleuropa".
    Grateful not to be dead, or frightened, or oppressed,
I think of the call in the song of the blackbird:
    When you patrol the dust of Mitteleuropa
It doesn't perceive that you and history are there;
    It sings with a voice that must be dreaming
It is a petal and so, rosily, all for free,
    In one cool fold of fire the petal wraps you.

Local Roads

These local roads they say
In Texas hug their curves
Or cracks and hollows
Like ancient pain

I looked ahead
I thought a turtle or what else
A flexing clump a shell
Had waddled half across

I ran to find if I was wrong
But there it was
Again the vacant womb
A god imagined human music from

My impulse the reverse
I slipped that hood back on
I shrank into the shell
To shield a scaly head

Whirled into the air I heard
Colossal whistling shoes
And fingers beating time
But vaguely on my back

Caught up with me at last
What century was this
My negligible weight
How balanced in his hand

Scars of ancient lightning
Scollop the vaulted shell
What if they broke open
What frenzy would he feel

A Portrait of J.L.M.

We called him spirit of the place,
But he's more like a good old tree root.
Went off, a year gone, back to Rockport.
It seems, when he'd gone, us not even
Knowing it, everything fell apart.
                    Wish I remembered

What he told me. This bit of town I landed in,
These railroad tracks he'd known, secret
Signs chalked on the freight wagon doors,
Hobos bivouacking, and how he'd drift across,
Talk with them. That was far back
In the Thirties, near enough to the yard on Seventh
He got our big old bamboo from, planted it.

        Wanderings, the split rail
Fences he built, him wiry then as now, bird faced,
Out west of Sanantone; any job he could find
He put both hands to. He belonged with
Boilers of big ships, blue clouds
Of working people on the move, tumbleweed;
You do the most you can.

        Far out hereabouts
He'd gone courting, before big money
Rolled the roads in. Remember now,
Hummed the tune once, he did. They walked out
Through live oaks together, rocks, and cedar,
Listening to the trickle of the creek in Spring.
He sat his Mildred down, kissed her,
Same old tune in their heads.

        I ate her cakes
She'd later bring at Christmas down the hill,
Stopping to chat a while, propped against
The doorpost, she'd laugh like anything
But sometimes she took ill.

        Drains, spigots, carburettors,
The pump, I saw his knuckles whiten
When he fixed them, and later his hand
Shook, breath caught, and as he worked
His mouth helped, with twists and lippings.

Rolled his own cigarettes; told me –
Here's this old song book, found it at the county dump,
You want it? 1865 – Irish songs. Irish
As his Indian scout grandfather had been. He'd
Told him of hilltops hereabouts

Where the Indians hunkered,
Yawning. And how a coach might rumble by,
Gold or guns in it, stuff they could use. And how
Into this cave his grandfather went once, deep,
Now they've blocked it, but it goes underground
All the way from the lake to Tarrytown.
A volcano, too, he said

I might not believe it,
Not so far off, east, he found obsidian there,
Beyond where the highrise banks and turnpikes
And the military airport are. Trees,
He loved trees and drove miles to see them
At their best, the right time of the year.
Buckeye and catalpa in their first flower,
Chinaberry, dogwood.

All birds had ordinary names,
Like redbird, but once in a while he'd speak
Old words, not from books but from Tennessee,

Like once he said "quietus". Always
Flesh in his words, and bone, and in his doings,
Not absent even from the way he'd knock
A bourbon back, straight, that was the way
He liked it, then roll another cigarette.

For Mildred when her teeth
Fell out he whittled deer horn so she'd have
A biting edge up front. When he came by, dressed
Smart for a visit, he'd be wearing false
Rat teeth up front and give a wicked grin.
There was this park he kept,

He knew all the weeds in it,
All, and told how some weed sent
Cows mad and was taken too much liberty with
By them young folks as went out there
For a high time.

Well, then he'd push off
In his battered pickup, headed for a honkytonk
Some place down the line. Why don't folks look at
That kind of man? Some say insight
Comes when you tell the individual
Get lost. What's all their deep droning talk
To him? He's too smart to think up
Revolutions, what's it, that perspective stuff?
Maybe he's nobody

But he made things work,
Never slaving, nor ginrollizing. Made things
Shift and level with every breath he drew.
Had no grievance, spoke no ill of anyone
Or anything save spindly offshoots
Of tree roots that split drainpipes in the country,
Having ballooned in them, like brains
Got swole, so he'd say, with all the excrement.

Woden Dog

1

Wot doth woden dog
Por dog drageth plow

Thing odd dog not
Much good plow drager

But por dog drageth
All same plow

More come jellifish
Sting him woden dog

Jellifish in air now
Other odd thing

A speeking maner come
Round back to trooth

So doth dog plow
Plant seed of tree

Por dog life short
Woden dog long hope

Woden dog keep stung
Jellifish all round back

Dog hope tree grow
Much tree grow soon

Dog want find tree
Find releaf releaf

2

Bus drifer pleez
Make a smoth start
If not woden dog fall over

Bus drifer stop graduel
If not woden
Dog hit deck

Pleez bus drifer
Tern corner sofly
Woden dog cant hold on

You no he cant sit
Propper
You no he cant holtite

Forgoet how to life has he
Lest thing nock him sensles
All you no

Woden dog smoth graduel
Woden dog sofly he scare think
You forgoet how to drife

3

Jakit off jus warin sox like mean you
Woden dog reed times ever doggone day
Nites watchin his toob wow
Haffin the noose hapn

Wow fokes I tel you
Woden dog lap up noose
Woden dog bominate seecrit he reely do
Noose noose he bark runnin down street
Galumfin baknforth to his malebocks

He wannit so bad
He wannit to go
Like choclit maltn ketchup
Hole globe pakitchn pree paredn paid fur
Sitn in his noose baskit

No seecrit make woden dog
Bust out in flour one mawnin
Lookit soaps he buy woden dogfood
Killins toon that po looshn stuf
Brung home in his teeth

Come days wen he skratchn say
Mite try killin sumwun to make noose of me
Paps if I make noose off him
He dont done do it?

Woden dog howcom you loss
Yor own seecrit eye sunshine
Woden dog howsit taist that woden dogfood
Whars thet kemel dog
Ever see canser wok a mile
Smokin up a kemel ever see war stop
Juscos you lookin?

Jeez fokes jus thort
If bad stuf stop no mor noose fur woden dog
Wot then ole flee bit dog
You see nuddin to lookat
You jus sit theren cry

4

Whodat
Striden backnforth in orifice
Who *dat*
Givin ordures

Whodat maken long biznis calls
Eatin long biznis bananas
He look horty
My whodat planifikting plitical fouture

Watchout
Here he come zoom by
Zoom silva jet clatter copta
Weekend in Toekyoe?
Meeting Younited Nayshun?

Whodat now
Widda dame in a yot wearing captin hat
Crakin lobsta
My my

Woden dog thats who
Woden dog how smart you done got

5

Hard inside
Woden dog

Woden dog gon
Sniff aroun for mudder

Mudder soft inside
Woden dog dig

Woden dog swetpant
Nudden come up

No mudder
Dipressed woden dog

Dog shrink gifm pill
How that now help

Dog body keep movin
But inside he nut

No mudder inside
No soft strong mudder

Nuddin in world
Woden dog size

Howls too purty offen
In his dog house dum

So small he feel
Stinkin wikid woden

6

Yes dern dawg
Urmpteen snarls
Makin nuddin
No bedder

You always countin
Countin crazy dawg
You mean
See me through glass

Derm yew lukn so glum
Like eny doods nuddin
Yew like like yew
Say dancein shit

Call yewsell a dawg
I aint buyin
Yew aint no morna
Cardbord ratlsnaik

Yew mean
Snarlin always makin
Fuss yew bossy think
Me mor stoopidn yew

Maybe too
But I countin
The timesnile git yew
Wunofem

7

Woden dog keep stil
So you can feel it
Movin

Rounanroun whirlin world
Why you keep with it
Is that reel

Woden dog
Keep stil so you
Can feel it movin

8

Hey now
Hoo done got hide
Inside you innerlekshuls

Meckin
Yore gin
Roll I say shuns

Hooz
Moovin yoohoo
All ways tokkin

Wokkin long
Rode like you wuz
Uh ginrollized creekin

Rekkernize hoo
He be my my if it aint are
Ole solom fren dubble you dee

9

Woden dog sittin
On the backstares

Sittin in the dark
Breathin a bit

What's this listen
Breathin

Laff
Woden dog

That's it
Laffin on the backstares

Thems wavesnwaves
Them cool backstares

Help dog floatin
Low float high

Not let waves go so
You seem zikazak

Doan it hurt some
Hey woden dog

Not let the laff hole up
In woden dog box

Listen breathin just so
Now no more done hurt

10

Wyso suddn everbody
Rite on walls

FREE WODEN DOG
Anifs time

Like I never got
Inclose free

Woden
Dog piksher?

Spose no place else
To rite

11

Silva smoak of pine
Burn chill
Woden dog shivver
Owl not heard

Lightslice fix to floor
Think dead
Woden dog like ice
In his box owl not heard

Owl hoot rainbow
Out of owl eyes
Owl hoot rainbow wonder
Dog not see dog bark at ghost

Owl not heard
Dog munch heap white aple
Not feel snow as owl bountie
Not smell snow rainbow

Woden dog eat heap
Aple up
Pip corn all cold aple meat
Not see owl

Not see some owl eyes
Not hear
How pips look sound yum yum
Crunch owl eyes aple up

Dog wine in boxn stay putn scoff
Woden dog alltime scoff
Woden dog shut in wod
Not smell sweet pine

Woden dog not smell wind song
Burn swingin low
Swingin in pine wod
Owl not hoot fur him in pine log

Owl not hear in dog box
He woden dog
Snow owl hoot that rainbow now
Now hootn touch dog heart

Jerusalem, Jerusalem

White building under pecan tree
Four poles cradle the porch roof

Beyond gap in branches blue sky trackless
Shingle roof slope beckons ghost of pagoda

White wall veined with leaf shadow
Tree unfolds a boom of spray

Homely air, who knows which way moving
Tree pulse drums, cricket whistles tune

Old walls of wood creak when air cools
Tree spoke to folks indoors a rustling lingo

Crisp lettuce on their plates and red meat
Perched in tree same bird sang as now

Pecan tree sole hero still grows
Slowly war and work fetched those folks away

Too bad house now gone to seed
In trashed rooms white devils hang out

Tending itself – a tree in majesty
Glued to gum, soda pop, the white mouth

Look again: no thought can be too high
Of whisper locked in white heart

Tell thought: still harder time ahead
Don't hold against them drift of old song

Coral Snake

I had been planting the sliced seed potatoes
When the snake started up from underfoot
And slithered across the gravel I stood on.

His beauty was not the point.
He was the kind that kills in a minute or two –
Chop off the finger he bit, or else.
But he was beautiful: alternating the black,
Red, and yellow rings more regular far, thick or thin,
Than wedding bands on a jeweller's ringstick.

He had come out of nowhere like evil.
He didn't care about me or want me.
I cared about him enough – it was fear,

Fear, not for me, no, but for him, the snake:
Long-trapped, an old horror breaks loose,
Later you say Alas, the snake was beautiful.
So I wonder what I can kill him with,
And notice in my hand the hoe; he isn't far,
Full stretch in his ringed ripples I see him
Slithering east of the two asparagus ferns.

I whop the hoe down and nail his head in the gravel
Between the chicken wire fence and a vegetable frame.
But he won't let go, I'm wrong, his free head
Rose over the quartz and flint pebbles;
Wild, the taut pure body, to be moving on and on.

Nothing to be done; if I shift the hoe
He'll streak through the chicken wire and I'll be
Cut off. I pressed harder on the hoe blade,
His tough coil resisted and the head
Wove a figure of eight in a pocket of air.

I didn't want it to be done, I didn't.
But how now to stop, considering his pursuits,
Easygoing as he is, pinheaded, slow to bite –
They say his tooth sits so far back
He needs to chew to do you in.

For there was more snake now in me than him.
I pushed the hoe blade harder down
And reached around the gate post for a stone.
That stone I eased
Beneath his tiny weaving head, taunting him,
Then reached around the post for a second stone.

When I looked again
The small black head with its yellow nape band
Was pointing up and the mouth, opening, closing,
Snapped at air to repel the blind force
Which held him down.

I could not do it, not to him, looking so
True to himself, making his wisdom tell,
It shot through me quicker than his poison would:
The glory of his form, delicate organism,
Not small any more, but raw now, and cleaving,
Right there, to the bare bone of creation.

And so I gripped the second stone but steadily
Thumped that telling head down flat
Against the surface of the first stone.
The broken body, I lifted it up and dropped it
Later into a vacant honey jar. The colours
Now have faded; having no pure alcohol,
I pickled the snake in half a pint of gin.

Wild Flowers

Like voices
They never grew in water;
All began with nobody there to see.
Warmth helped; mud propelled them; early
The seeds rode in animal pelts across immense
Reeling distances, or
Were blown through light by the wind,
Like lovers.

When we were bush mice
They settled, ignored, in the cooling places;
Blood took heat,
Bees ate them, lizards and happily
Spiders liked them. Lodged in the fat of horses
They travelled. Tigers, and us,
Still tree hoppers, hardly felt what colours
Ringed by unearthly
Fragrances without names they had.

Far off the glittering libraries,
Vases of blown glass;
But look,
On roadsides they exist. Songs in our hands
They go along with us. A passion
Means us to pick them, so
Responding to early light we stop; then drive on home
To draw blankets back
And make our love while sensing them,
Their far fields, their darknesses.

Svatava's Dream

Twice changed, forty years
Different country, different person

There I was, again, you must
Have heard me tell

How when I was eleven, all
The books of this old writer, how

Eagerly I read them, mystic, yet
Only now, back, beyond the river

Was I aware how close I was to him,
And found my way down cobbled

Lanes, twisting
Into his pink museum

Found some friends, a man, a woman
Had made a painting of the house

It was pink and breathing, walls
Went out and in, windows

Pink, the air was flowing out and
In again, I heard the sounds

The city sounds, just as ever
They had been, just as ever

But they said the house was mine
Mine if I wanted the pink museum

Yet the painting was my house
Here, not there, stone, this

House I live in, mine, of stone
It hurt me so to choose, I could not

Tell whose pink house was there or here
To be mine if I wanted

Was it for me, the old museum
The writer's mystical pink

And me eleven, was the picture
Where I am, or in a renovated

Hradshin room, was this a time
When you breathe fast and double

A time in the flush of being
A house you make with breath

Go pink and everything
For you are torn

The Turquoise

Somehow the memories fizzle out on us.
Large blank eyes of people starving.
A snatch of music soon
Will be Merida, the mirrored bedroom, not
The pang felt there, but a fountain
Touches palm trees. Pang –

I forgot how perception had to be
Wrenched from its
Regular socket: the speech of folds, eyewhite
And snow the robe a woman wore,
Foreign liquor
The smell of a man at noon in his hammock.

Raw stuff: a crooked
Line of objects. Look, it is put
Straight like hair by distance.
The whole shadow of (our tune) your smile
Oozed first from
Repetition on a jukebox. Careless

Memory cooks
The kind of meal you
Gulp down, because the right place
Had shut, or the old prices are
Out of sight. Compulsion
Turns you still

Back to the same town: the flies
In children's eyes are blue, the drowned
Horse prongs the air still,
Silver hoof; never sensing wrong,
The deadly salesmen frisk again
With girls in the disco.

Swat a fly, scratch the wall
Of an ear with a toothpick: four, suddenly,
The grouped figurines
Loom huge from the desk angle,
And glow, clay Chupicuaro, bronze
Krishna, the wooden African –

As gods. To construct them
Ancestors broke through their skins,
Getting this far at least: the rock
Crystal coyote, stud him
With turquoise, let the orange fire
Be a tail like a beacon;

For the unseen escapes,
The remembered
Dominion cracks, falsifies
Desire and presence as they fly screaming
Before us, headdress and tail
Bushy, slashing backward in the dark.

A Forge in Darkness

They hadn't forgotten his name
Or whereabouts the forge was,
The brick oven, hot glow
Of charcoal, the hammer floats
Up, held in mid-air now, and
What beer the old man drank.

A heart isn't like that. A heart
Won't wait until the dark
Comes to cool things off a bit.
It works through the blinding
Noon heat, careless of sparks,
Of hoofs clipclopping uphill.

Boys came by. Owls looked on.
A horse tail flicked at bluebottles,
Under the canopy of this pecan.
This hill – part of the night then,
A slope, that's all, crested with a forge,
Like a wave flecked with red foam.

What a letdown for her, hitched
To that limping, fretful man,
The reek of sweat and charcoal on him –
And her arms could take a whole sky in,
Her thumbs govern long ships or fondle lambs,
Yet she slid from her wave and under him.

It was here, right here, where I came
To be living. She's gone, he's gone.
I cook chicken where the forge
Must have been. In the dark I
Pour out more wine to remember
The little old lives of them.

Taking a chance, I think
That's where she must have gone:
Into the artifice of not forgetting
A name and what went on,
When the boys watched and owls
Heard the hammer come down.

Ancient Lace

Sitting silent and a long time gone
Hearing the tower clock strike faraway two
Feeling the sun toil in the skin of your face
Truth to tell waiting ain't so bad he said
Listen to the Carolina wren

Try not to let things ever get you down he said
Carolling like she found a roach to eat
Zucchini zucchini she call in the green bamboo
Tower clock won't ever strike a two the same he said
That's Emmy now knocking on a wood block

Or it's a kitchen pot she could be knocking on
The little changes bring you back to earth he said
No great shakes plain poor old earth he said
But now by heaven that was a woodpecker
Real weird it snickers with a hiccup

Don't always put your life on the line he said
A great shit heap out there and me and you
Leastways we settle up to be a whiff of it
Ten feet up today looking across the town
What speaks to you makes all the difference he said

Might be that little stick of frankincense you lit
Burning in the tree tub and a Carolina wren
And a stroke or two on a bell and a bird's note
It's good when things pierce your heart a moment
Make it pure he said and plenty more than heaven did

It's that warm the sun to melt your mask he said
And did they bring any wine for them to sip
So be it if they did not and enough's enough
Long time since like shooting stars they did set off
Suppose their whispering brocades will pass this way

Michèle's Rooms

The handle of the willow basket curving
The red tiled unlevel trodden floor
At knee height the clock face but no clock body
Toy clock hands constant at twenty to six

The wooden bowl empty of apples
Balls and hanks of wool in the willow basket
The procession of sea urchin shells on the mantelpiece
The angled needles as they pierce the wool

In coloured sleeves the shelved LPs
Loops of plants I came to water
Pink of the wool and of the towering candle
Snowy bear and rabbit warm for Lola

Rising suns of scallops knitted into a shawl
The way the shawl hangs unoccupied from a hook
A mobile by the window strung with wands and ducks
The tang of wine a moment held between the teeth

The invisibility of the hook
The absence of electricity
The plant bowl that overflowed on the telephone bill
The tiny bird crouched on the mantelpiece

The lifted latch and the opening window
The breeze that burrows through a shirt for flesh
All these marks to detect her laughter by
The word's very event in a special voice

Curve of the beak of the sacred ibis
Heart of legend locked in a nondescript replica
Spheres that only come to thought as curves completely seen
Two cracks in the wooden beam darkening them

The wooden beam's edges bevelled by an old axe
Absent from the encyclopaedia the surge of the scribe's mind
Flit of the pen's tip crossing two scraps of paper
The ghostly scribe without a name

Another Almost

Almost it might be better
to forget the past than build
ruins out of ruins

Perhaps the ruins are forms
of a response too blocked or timid.
Who can figure a whole house?

Think of the first scavenging Turks,
incurious, they patched their huts
with odds and ends of temples

No, I mean it is tough going
always to remember
so little or too much

Then have it all, or some,
spring unbidden back into place.
The bundle of woe is heavy

Wave to me as I go,
inhabitants of memory,
from your ruins, houses, forests

Continue the story that broke,
somehow, in the middle.
Let me see, let me smell you

Intact to my hearing
perhaps you will open
zones of being I never knew

Mysterious flesh
might blossom, lost hills
tipped with frail churches

Mansions complete
with moats of liquid silver,
misty kitchens, whence

Incredible pastries issue, baked
in ovens I never saw,
wines I never drank

Might redden tables of real oak
in twilight courtyards –
all ordinary as now. So I bend

With an ache for you, child,
and one for you, my only love,
and another for Doyle, Irish pilot

Blown to bits on a rocket range.
More lovely or horrible
things I know

Happen to others,
I write this only to shorten
the time of a music

Which, unless I forget,
will mass ruin on ruin.
The watermill we slept in,

My other love, the rushing
water beneath us,
you had clipped my fingernails

So I forget it, forget, child,
the midnight we were frightened of.
I hoist on my back again

The bundle of woe, but first
I open it, a crack,
to see the bloody rags

And worn-out toothbrushes,
the splinters of bone
and a silver ring from Afghanistan

Which slid into a river;
I sniff the hair beside me,
I touch excited midnight skin

The time of a music
almost now I hear the spell of it
playing backwards

A Revenant

Now she is here
Again, quick, in a taste
Of lemon, not even so
Much as a bite, she is here
In a whiff

Of lemon peel, no way
Even to tell
Where from, the light
Saffron perhaps, a snowy
Touch of metal

Or, afloat
On a flood of being, me,
I had drawn
A tingle out, indistinct,
A distant signal

Flashing in the hotter rush
Of air tonight, mixed
Into it, funny
Today, the wiggle
Of a child, head back

Shrimp bodysock, she
Did a glancing
Noonday
Dance across
A crack

In a paving stone, she
Shook
At the sky
Her fist
With a flower in it

Now so long dead
Another
Is here, I remember to be
In the taste
Or touch, or in the child

A wandering
Sensation, mutely
To learn my shape, later to flit
Ghostwise from a being
I will never know

Cybele

It is cold outside so she has walked in
Loving my feet for her own good reasons,

Straight in, tail up, scanning the kitchen
She discovers nothing but a desire

So at my feet she winds and unwinds
Her calico skin. When I tap on the blotter

Up she lifts a paw, forgets, listens again,
Looking elsewhere, if elsewhere is anywhere

And curls in a fit of abandon
Around the tongue of my tennis shoe.

Her paw milks the lace, her paw milks the ankle bone,
Amorously unparticular she forgets her milk

Habit, suddenly crouches, licking her tail:
Suddenly I know nothing for her is sudden

For she forgets her forgotten tail, silent
She explores cavity, cavity, for instance

Behind the cutting block propped against
The wall, she has found a fascination

Shadow or moonlight there, scampers off
In a rage of vague desire for shadow

And foot, the raw smell of shadow and foot,
She's stepping over hollows everywhere

And finding what she wants to be hidden there,
Everything new, glistening cushion, clay

Horse, fragile, over it she has to step
A soft way. What invisible spasms of being

Span her heart beat? How come she detects
Here in this room the moon she only knows

From green by the shadows moon-eye makes
Nothing of? Smells are shape, the sharp

Outline of mouse, the cry of yucca white
She evidently smells when tasting my feet.

Not my feet. Them, me she ignores. It is
A very sweet crisis to be constantly cat:

Her senses, precise as Gieseking's fingers,
Track a music, her veins are shivering with it –

Transformation, the furnace of horror
Red in her claw, fact in her leap of fire –

She is arrow, target. The bird, a flit
She hesitates to hear, could prong her

Against a sky that is no sky for her
But promise of open, beak, edible, never

Depressive, it stings, strikes, white glistens.
Bone aches too that way in my meat.

A Farewell in Old Mexico

Perhaps her husband was the engineer.
Palm up, timing perfect,
She waves to him. A hazel wave.
Here is the hand she cups, at the limit

Of an arm's curve, to catch his sooty kiss.
Animal black complex of intestines
Afloat on a thunderhead of steam, to the clank
Of twenty open trucks, you expelled

A hiss. Soon the sunflower field of faces
Lifts as one to swallow cool sierra air.
Wind sang star patterns into the grit.
On the boardwalk begonias inhabit tin cans;

Liquid, they are mirrored, even redder
In the sweat beading her top lip. The caboose
A dot, now she waves, with her comical
Sense of order, to it, not him.

La Morena

My white cow tonight is quite silent
My white cow milking a heart from darkness

What tricks and silks will she tumble into
My white cow with opening parachute lips

My white cow with a shirt of woodsmoke
My white cow with a beehive of desires

Sometimes an abandon seizes her by the horns
Sometimes she is placid and sings in church

My white cow dancing in her field of fire
My white cow walking with dangerous steps

Everywhere she supposes there are cathedrals
Everywhere bells inscribe on air their spiral signs

My white cow with marked ideas of her own
My white cow whose tuft is a tangle of tempers

The baskets of air hang from her solid bones
The jugs of earth lift with her little breasts

My white cow who makes sorrow burn a day away
My white cow who makes sorrow bite like a shark

My white cow who shivers and penetrates men
My white cow who rides men bareback

Often conscious of too many things at one time
Often come times when she knows nothing at all

She has no clock for her timing is internal
No voice but hers alone tells her when and how

She will eat dry bread if there's none better
My white cow who tastes always of oranges

My white cow who goes one better than the snow
Her quim is heaven for whom she pleases

In the nights we stretch with furious argument
My white cow takes every word to its limit

Shortening days we walk together hand in hand
More than once she tore my arm from its socket

I will do my dance one-armed for my white cow
I love her life her ways her difficult nature

We live beneath roofs that stand centuries apart
My white cow in small towns and purple cities

My white cow in a village dances to the guitar
My white cow sipping wine from a cup of clay

When the baskets are hanging bright in the water
They fill with her fish and creak in earthquake

When in my white cow's hair old stories are told
We stop them to start the world afresh redeemed

She is absent in the canyon of her red lust
She is present in the ordinary dishes we eat off

My white cow is a black one to tell the truth
Or else Chinese or else some kind of Arabian

To call her a cow at all is a profound mistake
She is a leopard with four cubs in a forest.

My white cow in that hotel stripping off her clothes
My white cow who is not mine at all

My white vanishing cow with her dolphin legs
My white cow who wades *toute nue* in the Toulourenc

Her skin mirrors itself and that is it for us
I fall into her skin to oblige Lord Shock

I tongue my white cow in her purity and playfulness
She will never come around to believing I mean it

My white cow imagines me far off running away
Little does she know I run to catch her leaping form

White cow who dances wild in the middle of the world
White cow your sweet dust with the wind blowing over it

Night Wedding in Anamur

Cézanne made men to play bézique
    You look at heavy backs
A hatted peasant head
    Perhaps a pipe gone out
Bonehard still though fathoms deep
    The wily roosters winged by hazard
Shine in the cottage empire of paint

All that was a scene will change
    The table on a shore collects
A foreign gaze a touch far out
    A table clothed in Turkish white
Seven people sitting at it
    Finger rings and tulip heads
Formal around the bowls of salt

Now let the scene unfold their flesh
    Night opens wide its cobalt mouth
Smoke and smells are tucked away
    So black the ovals cane sombreros blow
Across the sand they taste of olive

A fresher wind can levitate them now
    It has them float
The fish mothering sea that never wastes
    A breath when day dawns or doomed
Civilizations cut their bonds to fall apart
    That selfsame sea poises on its crests

Musicians busy thoughtful witnesses
    A heartbeat above
The old as usual unrolling ocean scrolls
    Now mould the air with such sweet force
Again the table lifts and dancers
    Leaping coupled skim the water

Bathed in her moon the bride
    Heavenly arms outspread
Dances to the upbeat
    And she so startled looking like a corpse
Strung with fairylights and coppery balloons
    Still quickening Attis torn and underground

Her table is upheld
    Ghosts around it eating – fast
(Softly out of her silken box she rose)
    With lamb and water melon
Froth of beer still ticking in the glasses –
    Each a singular shadow out

Circle

They all run around the doorstep
They point at the sky
And for sure the stars are falling
So many it's like the tassels
Of an oldtime dancing dress

But why look
When lost in thought
Inside

Why, if someone you are thinking about
Once in a house long gone without a trace
Might be recalling now
The way rain would start to patter
Across the timbered roof

And in the palm of her hand
How the dog's muzzle felt
The wet nose clean
The tongue warm

Ballad of Charlotte

Before she bought the knife to kill Marat
Charlotte Corday had bought a fancy hat.

The five-inch knife she bought at a hardware store;
The hat was black with ribbons green galore.

At a hardware store she bought the five-inch knife,
Resolved to take the gutter tyrant's life.

She bought the hat to do the thing in style,
With a sort of Norman Mona Lisa smile.

Consider, when you visualize the scene –
Over his lukewarm bath she had to lean:

What if across her eyes the hat had slipped,
Unsighting her the moment when she gripped

Violently the knife, to push it in?
Or if the hat had fallen past her chin

And plopped, before she pushed, into the water . . .
Marat and Charlotte both dissolved in laughter.

Due to her sense of style it was not so;
She does for history what she had to do.

Out of her dress she takes the knife – one thrust,
Her blade has pierced his body, as it must.

Later the questions. Charlotte acted 'alone'.
Was 'firm' and 'feminine'. Conspirators? None.

Her motive? Folks, I struck the monster dead
To frighten other monsters off, she said.

Marat, mean-spirited, vindictive, shrill
Poseurs like you defraud the hungry still.

Ranting fanatics cast you as a martyr.
If only Charlotte's hat had hit the water.

Charlotte instead is later to be seen
Riding a cart on the way to the guillotine.

Behind the cart, voices sang a song,
Tiny voices heard, but not for long.

The scarlet robe she wore, without her hat,
Showed all her body's curves. Now why was that?

Pelting rain had soaked her to the skin,
No doubt to purify her of her sin.

Whose were the voices? Little girls, they say,
Held hands and sang and danced for that Charlotte Corday.

The Balcony Tree

New neighbour say: hope it won't interrupt you
When I walk by your open door?
O no, I say: I'm really not a rat,
At least not so you'd notice. Spring and Fall
Open is the way I like to leave it.

Hung, too, from the balcony tree a bird feeder.
New neighbor say she like it, kinda neat.
Little tree in leaf now. We
Hope this alley cat won't find
Ways to catch a finch, or me, the rat.

We say: before we open doors, we'll watch
For finch or sparrow. If they be there,
We won't step out to do the things we do.
Won't switch on our sensitive ignitions.
Try not to scare the creatures from the tree . . .

Must say, though, I miss
The earlier neighbour, long before
I chained the feeder to a branch.
Miss her mad look, her finger tapping window,
Clothes gone, I miss the skin, the Latin

Nipples in the candlelight,
Miss the swoop and sweat of her sassy back,
Her talk, till she took off, still going on.
Did she find work, make a buck
Where she went, with her perfumes, to look for it?

Or is she fat in San Antonio and fed up?
Who else betrayed her, made her?
Under the tree, with a low hopeless laugh
She coiled her hair up once like a Tarahumara.
Not so my new neighbour:

She tells me there's a gap. Events
To be explained. Touches of understanding
Shunned in fright. Her smile, like a fan
She tries to open but can't find the catch.
What can I tell her?

Jump the gap? Snail has a place to go,
Horse, quick, rumbas over copperhead?
But whole creeds have collapsed into the banks
We borrow lifetimes from, to eat
Frenzy, evacuate abstraction –

New neighbour know it all. So I say:
You made it home, and here is being –
No reverend killers ring this balcony tree,
My door, no bullet whanged it yet, I close
Only when I sleep or hear them march by.

Walking the Puppy

The poet of the abyss
Takes to walking the puppy
While scrolled waves gather shape
To pound the shore
He sees a flowing violet web whisked from the abyss
Furrow the hump of a sea shell

Gentle frenzy puppy digs
Through the salt and oil
She hopes for a smell at least of something
Her quick young claws how like the waves
How like her pelt the shooshoo of the foam

They frolic away to a dry dune
Where gulls glide on down to meet their shadows
Wind lets fly its foibles round the clock
Cooling the backs of nondescript objects

A bottle top, an inch of ocean macaroni
Yield a howling O
Yield an M for the Mothers
How can a puppy interpret such a text
Will she be able to scratch from it a whiff of the real

Soon the night, night will drift over it all
A violet web of swoops and ribbons
And giving tongue to other stars
Breath by breath Delta will begin to expand
Still with beaks to pierce the wind gulls are marking time
Others trot on twilit stilts looking pretty stupid

Even the puppy waits for the poet to catch up
Patting her head he forgets what it means to breathe
He strokes her small throat
In love with every shining grain of sand
He is hungry for her small head and kisses it

She runs in the shining, golden dog, mad with delight
Though at a distance, nervous of course
One small hand brushing the hot heavenly blood away
The other cupping her loneliness
Aphrodite walks from the waves again

Vietnamese Harp

Before first light awake
    At a touch on a button
One taut steel string plucked I heard
    And another, another

Penetrating the dark a music
    Of spine and thighbone
Clear as the contour of a water lily
    Ghostly as the snow it cups

Floated from its peak
    To ground, a shimmering pagoda
Spreads and folds its wings
    Stands where I lay

Amazingly nowhere, almost
    Too much trance for a body
So soon in the day, cut loose
    From the singing zigzags

I walked outside, by the open window
    Taking the same sounds in
But curious who in spirit
    Now might weep to be listening

Saloon with Birds

If someone barefoot stood in a saloon,
His dromedary might be chomping, outside,
That majestic meal. High olive notes
Plucked from a mandolin. Fumes. Leafgreen.

A dark descends. There, with banana palm,
Consorts forbidden music. Ugly. Ocean.
Delay it. First a clatter, from the birds.
They wax decrepit. Vocal signatures:

Who could ever have so illuminated them
That the letters, cut from stark air,
Assume no solitary monumental pose,
But wavily ache with the boat hulls?

Certain or not, an urgent finger prodded
Epsilons and wagtailed gammas free
From habit, a peculiar glue. No help. No
Waste. In the saloon each dust spake.

In the saloon the spokes of another
Sunlight, still this ocular companion though,
Rolled afternoons around, like meatballs,
Bubbles of corn sizzling in a crystal pan.

Throaty owls also, they could entertain
Quick, tensile teeth. A joy. Pelican moonlit.
Look at a pine nut. It exists, you know.
Little furred insects inhabit vast smells.

For this the saloon is open. A waft.
A waft is all it takes. A venetian blind
Has wrinkled the wash basin. A cool expounds
Blood orange, air in China, appalling beliefs.

Air wraps the mast. Air singing. Air,
The solo invader who timed anew
Our free objects. The saloon twangs,
Dust swims, a gong letting its hum fly.

Closing never. Least of all on syllables.
A split lemon has released from evil
Any soul what's willing. Get that. Now
Never you move like you were shrunk to be.

Or else forgo the little sorrow. Treasure
The big one. Tell, in the saloon,
Nothing of it. Look up. Long enough
The ocean has delayed. You can breathe again.

The Headland

Beyond the shacks where food is sold
Beyond the booths haunted by carpet men
Beyond the goats and stone lidded broken tombs
Look the headland

How many times have you seen it there
Not knowing if it had a place in time
Thinking you had seen it only in a dream

Beyond any imaginable midpoint of the world
Memory brimmed unbidden with whole colours
Only to end in a choking dust of names

But answering your body which stores light as it can
Answering rhythms that curl but cling to nothing at all
Rhythms given flesh for a measure to feel with

The track goes up on the shoulder of the headland
Saffron earth anchored by rock
Storm torn rock walls to clamber over at the top

How many times did you see from there
Sheltered in a bay the next village
Fishermen stooping at the prow to pull the anchor up
It would have taken a lifetime to get there
How many lifetimes to the city of emerald and snow

How many times hearing a mast creak
Hum of rope drawn taut and dripping
Did you look back to see the headland disappear

Shoe soles worn thin by long walks
Pierced by the long thorns
Then barefoot and kneedeep in the sea
Hardly ever any deeper
In your dented helmet or coonskin cap
There today again and glad but not to be alone
Shading your eyes you will have seen the headland

The Clothes Moth

Little as the fingernail of a ten-year-old,
You have the shortest whiskers of a cat.

Up close, easily seen in the slant light,
Two profiles merge, like rivers, across your wings;

And the face of a Chinese emperor is disclosed,
Smiling, moth, on your Mesopotamian back.

Outlined against the pinewood table top
Your shape is less fan, less tulip

Than the Egyptian lotus with tornado lips
They hammered into drachmas on Cyprus once.

So much abstruse cutting of throats then,
Now the history scatters in golden dust

I catch my breath at, when your whiskers twitch.
A breath lofted you, now gone you are,

Yet I think you might have been there always,
There no less than fingers I will fork to grip

The cigarette, than wine still black in a bottle.
What if now I saw the design on my own back?

What rivers, what profiles, what bloodshed
Might melt into a design to be misread,

As if through valley mist, by a yokel pretending
To an imperfect, imaginary intelligence?

Cloaked in provocative scrawls the globe
Throws to the winds the grids we put around it.

So, in the moment of this furor, you took off:
You wisely muscled in to my thin stock of wool;

Now I hear your soft jaws munch my blanket.
So I became your fleece and you my Argonaut.

A Huapango for Junius Avitus

Accedit lacrimis meis quod absens et
impedentis mali nescius, pariter aegrum
pariter decessise cognovi, ne gravissimo
dolori timore consuescerem.

— Pliny the Younger

[Note: Huapango – a Mexican dance-song of Caribbean origin, in which the dance steps of a couple alternate between trampling on one spot and hopping in a low arc to trample on another spot. Junius Avitus – died young, soon after becoming a senator, a protégé of Pliny the Younger, who loved him for his promise, his meticulous hard work, his willingness to learn (*Letters*, VIII, 23)]

1

Stepping out from the new Bangkok Café
Digesting the whitest
Meat of spicy chicken

Night hawk heard aloft
Orbiting the ventilators
Of Congress Avenue, this hot hot gulch

His high, strangled cry
A soprano raspberry
Reminding me of Rossini

Whom ice cream polished off
Boom – how come I slow down slightly
Firefly from split concrete winking

Cooks, octets and chickens
How come I slow down at all
All too soon will have had their fill of me

Boomboom boom – unwinding silver ladder
None too soon
Mysterious dame thou penetratest me.

2

Staring at the moon a cat thinks
It is a dish of milk

The cat staring at the moon
Wants to include it somehow

It might be cheese with a mouse
Tremendously creeping up on it

I'll wait and see, the cat declares
The same as I say this about the cat

The urge is there: live without knowing how
Idea is there: for building shrouded systems

Tear off the sheet: what's there is featured
Stone or a royal sport of the unconscious

A point in time – rounded arms reaching out
With heat but no direction, say Come over here

Your aftershave is nice, I'll risk the consequences
Vague, outside, still the traffic roars

At leisure sea shells unwind their echoing forms
Silver in the moonlight fox fur crackles

And crystal fleets whizz oblivious across the bridge
Their juggler, hands behind his back, distracted

A point in time split into infinitely small
Sensitive fibres could tomorrow resume

Existence as a hero, scribbled fish: I exist
Like everybody, waiting for a rhyme or crash

To work the change, a crisis freshening the sun
Yet suppose the sea shell, suppose the idea

Unqualified create only to disregard
Those singular fables which invent the cat

Uncontainable web, trembling with just what?
Whatever frenzy knits bones, whatever tenderness

Desires you to speak, on me your lingo's lost
You might pronounce wrath, or mercy, or both

You might shield me with ignorance
Rage at me for love I want to shake you with –

And how apt, settling under the baobab, the leopard
A dervish hat completes the cook who plays the spoons

You turn right
    at the second sign, soon, at the crossways
      of a bridge and a sea shell
        continue left to the cook
and straight ahead to the rhomboid of distraction

You will find a wing there
    and a corkscrew ascent
      to a second bridge. Do not miss the egg,
        clearly marked, you have been there before
and the lights give out, see, just before the dip

There is a field of cows,
    you pass it on the left
      the pylon, like a picked
        albacore backbone; if you stop
you'll hear the wind bellow in it, likely as not

Later, left at the fork
    and follow the loop. You'll smell woodsmoke
      if you're on track. Slow down
        at Silken Ladder, circle
Cat Lagoon, then back off and sleep some

There's a tidy walk ahead;
    the path is one you won't miss.
      Cobwebs will catch your shoes and face,
        the first aren't poison, but watch
for the purple ones, the stickiest, they mean forget

The Greater Evil.
  Now all the sounds will keep you
    wide awake: the nosing, quibblous, of the fong,
      click of bullwits, the oom's horn.
You'll soon tune in. Forward to the fork, here,

Or there, for the nth time,
   you have to decide –
      stop till sunup, or fail –
         plod on, dance with your telescope, tongs,
your feathering tool, your grip of loose leaves –

Plod on, soon you'll see the
   gap in the boob trees.
      Then (inaudible words)
         (more inaudible words)
Brisk wind foretold it, boom, the unshrouded sea

Here all things turn
   their backs on you. Nothing
      watches you. Now it is too late
         to save your precious skin, it's
listening the other way, as if to another voice

The load of *la matière*
   and feelings that attach to it,
      the great dusts, groans, the golightly trees
         turn inside out, reform into a hole
and in the hole (involved, turning its back on you –

Or can it be Death Mountain?) moment dwells.
   Let everything go, gaze at it,
      as long as it is there, the moment hole.
         Never think all time is abuzz in it.
Never put your eye so close you could be blown away

By the grace it is giving out, pulse
   never spent, of carnal
      starlight a fountain, supposing earth
         and you, if ever again, eye to eye with a beak-
to-flower hummingbird, can figure time like that

4

Soon is a kind of never in reverse
Save when a phrase's gist is negative
Soon you'll die just when you want to live
A cry from Never posits to disperse

Spun like a top in umpteen kinds of time
Configured as in music or more flat
As lurching on from this dull urge to that
Ugly history leaves a trail of slime

A soon that could be now the future past
Emergent time tormenting in the rose
Skipping an aeon if the ground's too hot

Ah incandescent now again outlast
Soons that never sang a note but froze
To dwindle on the tips of tongues forgot

5

My heron has flown into the blue night wood
My sparrow into the perpendicular dust
My falcon, better than my wrist, loves the sky

What shall I do, mysterious dame, with this thought
It has angles and nodes I know nothing of
I am not very well acquainted yet with the dark

I am not afraid of the night wood, nor of dust
And I love the sky no less than my falcon does
With a pinch of salt I eat food as I need it

Also I hear in corners floorboards creak
As if somebody trod behind the shadows there
But I do not collect my times into a pattern

I do not work things out or drink white milk
Because white things are impersonating me
A white horn in a corner blows for a minute

A white horn in a corner when the creaking stops
Spreads a vista of stone gates and streaming hair
In an ancient city where I met you sometime

And the city to come is a far cry from my thought
The generation of thought a far cry from reason
When I see my falcon's face I am not in doubt

There are skies
There are dusts
There are losses we bear as best we can

There is an old book on the demons I might read
There is a new face to love, which I do not choose
There is a distraction from things and anxieties

It is for instance distracting to know this or that
And how not knowledge hurts but experience
And how you live, mysterious dame, in death

It is distracting never to be disenchanted
To have the spring of joy always bubbling up
To be sad without any thought of sadness

Distracting to be told your sadness was intended
Sadness the snout of a weapon pointed at life
Heron, sparrow, falcon falling from the sky

The tone, of an unfingered string
The fluidity, now, of the flight
The going on of everything at your ancient behest

Come to me again with understanding some other time

Ballad of the Putrefaction

The poem of hateful persons hot in his mind
He met the girl whose work was to roll in creosote
Himself he wanted to set fire to the hateful persons
Nobodies governing nations without any sense of what's what
Not victors but victims of their spooks and greeds

Those were to be the subjects of a poem which began
The moment he walked into one of their oblong hotels
He smelled the frowst of power they had left behind
People not born for power but victims of it
Who spray around the scene like tomcats their fear
The poem began but was interrupted by fresh sounds

A tongue moved in a sticky mouth and a snowflake fell
Those were calls from pigeon throats in the courtyard
This was a finger brushing the skin of a tambourine
These were the dawning sounds he heard
When the power of hateful persons first crawls in the dark

Himself had been interrupted by collecting impressions
The kind of work he would have been quarantined for
In a world controlled by the hateful persons
My work is rolling in creosote among carpets
The pools of creosote stick to my hair and skin
And my skin peels off when I wash the creosote away

Himself was interrupted by me when he saw me roll
He called me over asking why I had shaved my hair off
He gave me a fourteen dollar bill for the taxi ride
We should have supper he said at the Kim Kim
A Chinese Turkish restaurant on the lower East Side

So himself was interrupted by a girl with no hair
And the poem of hateful persons came to a stop
But still what made his flesh creep was their peeve
The smell of the "lounge" where they brooded destruction
The carbon script of a menu they ordered fishes from
The pop of a cork as it quit their bottle of Sekt
Fear in their bones fitting them snug in the world's night

Then the blackbird began to sing in the courtyard
For at first light still he did not sleep
Phantoms of hateful persons pushed their faces
Across the twilight between him and me
Again he saw the squat bronze tractor woman
Straighten her headscarf in the hotel garden
Their monuments he murmured their long knives
Hack out the tongues of nightingale persons
Their slug fingers sign contracts for weapons

Typically one who ordered a total change of trees
Resenting the way leaves tore loose from a sycamore
Himself too mumbled how their language formulaic and glib
Formulaic and numb and belittling gave rhetoric a bad name
Mouse grey their claptrap squeaking in machines

But we got along and my lips were clear of creosote
I only interrupted our long kiss to tell him You amaze me
If he forgot me it was the fault of a blackbird
Interrupting the poem of hateful persons at first light
Another moment and I will see him again
Free of his gang of hateful persons and police
He said they live secretly in fortified estates
And don't know beans about the hunchback in the belfry

So the poem will shine through air in the darkest places
So its voices will banish the fug they spread
Sunk in plush chairs or stiff at their tank parades

But again it is me the creosote girl who interrupts
We have escaped across many adjoining rooms
And arrive in a crypt where police wagons park
Waving our fourteen dollar bill we must fly on
Because the shooting will never stop it seems
Up and down streets we zigzag through fields of fire
He has told me he knows where the Kim Kim is
What if I doubt himself more deeply now than he can

The Old Tour Guide – His Interpreter

He says there is a Greek house in Mustafapasha,
He says you go down a winding stone staircase
Into a crypt. On more stairs down to a crypt
Beneath it, a secret door opens. Now
There is more to be said, it seems.

I think he is saying that a blue sun
And utter stillness enfold the numen:
He says that in a third crypt under the second
A Christ of Sorrows stands alone, his face
Preserved in the original paint. That the face,
He says, illuminates all memory of the house,
Once you have been there, for your lifetime,
Is not certain.

What was he saying next? He says they found
A lost valley, by chance, two summers gone.
Conical churches there contain sealed tombs,
Full of treasure. Present, for anyone to touch,
A desiccated loaf, on an altar, a curled up
Sandal, each of substance
Evidently shunned by mice.

Now he says there are many places
Not to be gone to. Memory has no desire
To be disappointed. But, he says, nothing,
Nothing stops you wanting to go there.

He is describing the valley, how across
Its clear stream, from one willow bush
To the next, singing warblers flit: the bird
Called popularly heaven bird can be seen there,
Crested, with blue wings, throat of rose,
Best heard at noontime when it flutes alone.

That is what I think he said. In his thick
Local accent now he is saying this:
You must not cut loose from here and now,
Both hands taking hold have to pull, he says:
Let the crypt call to you, as the long road did,
Let the valley track the turning of your eyes
And always haunt the here and now you see.

That is the gist. Wait, what wild talk is this
Of war striking a far country . . .

                         Stored at home his great bow?
Seven times I heard the suffix
Which in his language indicates hearsay,
The saying a matter of doubt to the sayer,
Critical things might happen to have been
Otherwise.

                         Ah yes, he says,
Ah yes, this is the country of people after midnight;
Few have spelled out into the pleasure of a heartbeat,
Into a knot of mind, once and for all,
The loops of light they see spreading at sunrise,
The braid that snakes down a girl's bare back.
When we go to see what is there to be seen,
The knots and braids easily slip;
We learn to know how little we understand.

But as we go I believe he is saying
May Allah lift the griefs from all of us.

Skaters in the Luxembourg Gardens, 1909

    Black on white, figures astride a frozen pond,
    Long shadows travel, forms unfreeze the distance.
    A clock high on the palace façade has stopped.
    It is five to one, or else it is eleven.

    Suppose there was that year no bombing season,
    Though while snow drifts blew into Saint Sulpice
    A ghost bicycled through them firing pistol shots:
    However it was, here is a lull in a bubble.

303

Ankles turning as they try to move,
Two of the women wear such ponderous hats.
Shaping her mouth, narrowing her eyes
Another shoots an ecstatic look, at what?

Yes, a mouth can turn lips in like that
When ice absorbs a pond, air blows jawbones cold,
But *le dimanche* has arrived, the Galeries Lafayette
Set free their great bosomed girls.

Knees flexed and gliding from his corner
A waiter makes the scene, white shirt cuff
Circles the end of the longest arm on earth;
And the women giggle, this could be something else.

At the line of bowler hats behind them, not a glance;
Of the grudge fuming into the hat crowns, not a whiff.
Those bowlers heat old soldier headbones knit
In the semblance of a wound, raw, roughly sutured.

No use trying to tunnel back, they say.
Still you try it, drawn to any secret place.
Still the waiter fills his coat, not yet blown away
In a dugout; old fogeys crack a smile.

Webbed with hairlines the wafer of glass
Off which this print slid
Vaguely into the bluebell air of Spring in Texas
Eight decades almost after the event

Is in your lips, image intact;
The scratches hold their accidental ground
And are at home in the picture;
The people smile, humdrum in their hats.

Kin to them, rose Renoirs glow through the shell
Of the palace; air attends Fokine and *The Firebird*;
Five canvas women rolled under Picasso's bed
Have chosen who shall wear the masks and dance.

Yet unforefelt another ice was catching up on them.
Soon it will split even this mole's backbone.
Where do the long shadows else come from, and the light,
The sweep of light brightening that girl's face?

Monet's Weeping Willow

Involuntarily
    Microbes
In a drop of water
    We see what they cannot

A carousel
    The unbelievable
Speed of echoed
    Colours wheeling

And reel to seem
    To be seen weeping
Inside a single
    Unimportant tear

Or (duck in gunsight
    Fluting across the Danube
Delta at sunrise)
    A tot of eau-de-vie

Through its liquid
    Walls refracted
The cosmos calls
    Hallo goodbye

The Gardener in the Basilica

The gardener in the basilica, he stoops
To cut and lift the grass roots;
Little billhook in his grip he hacks what sprouted
Round the odds and ends at random:
Broken fluted column, writing,
A coffered rose, a marble sun.

While he cuts he whistles.
Same tune, over and over. Headscarf in the wind,
Down his back it flutters. Then he stoops,
As if born bent double. Face down,
He only sees a blur of marble forms;
He smells the wild pig smell of grass,
And smelling it he knows the weight of time.

Headscarf fluttering, hood of flame, fed by resin,
Colour of the buried time, round his head,
Hidden in it.
Never to be restored. Timbers creaking,

Low in the water, black on violet, home,
A galley anchors. Fingertips have tooled
In hammered gold an olive leaf. Deer leap
And the dolphin. Likely tales
About a god
Born flesh and bone taunt the peregrine soul,

And him, robed in his dust, perilous
Round his head that long
Gone Ionian autumn, him hacking,
Stooped, whistling, over and over
The same tune.

Fishing Boats at Assos

1

Goodbye bastions Aristotle squinnied at:
Over the hill I have to go, scorched
By a thought for the purposeful
Multitude building you, and down to the cool
Spread shadow of an ilex, phantom, no,
Barbarian to your bronze people.

                                        Goodbye
Delight among the drums of stone,
Once temple columns being lifted up
To civilize your mammoth headland –

                        And from her cabin,
Softly speaking, a girl steps, white lace
At her fingertips.

2

As ash flies from the tip of a cigarette
Into the harbour water
Moon on moon has risen and will set –
                                        They disappear,

The purposes; we disappear
Among the gunwales, capstans, grunge, lapping;

Lemon crescents on their scarlet,
Flags droop, solitary lights – flicker of a look,
How many smokes ago,

First a shock, then a script
Hook, line, and sinker penetrating you –
Sprint across the water. So does love.

3

Steady now, snowy in arc-light
The loop of a gnat
Did not collapse the model of its whim,
                              A shooting star.

Purpose begins when a blind will takes
A hold on time, toils then to perfect
An image of its matter; aspires in good faith
To provide; persists through loss,
Must keep going till it melts into mind:

Süzül oynak dalga . . .

                    Drifts of time,
Heaving poison cake, layer on layer,
                              Secret in the seen –

Tell me, Lord, to walk to you across the water

4

Canopies flap again, to fresh paint on a prow
The moon tries to pin a medal; the harbour
You could cup in a hand forgets for a minute
How distant, how old it is: everything ripples,

Dazzles, gives. Next, the phenomenal
Winking fabric clicks shut, and, trapped,
A mole thought can mutter only
"Hallo, now here's a thing."

5

A surge of joy
Suddenly remembering a blue light,
The shiver of it over the scales of a mackerel,
Warmth of an oar gripped
By fingers far bonier; then curious
Warrens you dug with tooth and claw
In sand; and freshest –

The first morn makes pristine
Bastions glisten;
Ovals of air flute one huge
Here-we-are hosanna with a scent
Of bread and woodsmoke,
Pinewood and excrement.

6

A silver griffin
Struck into a tetrobol, forepaw raised,
Passes from hand to hand:

Where now, with knapsack and Canon,
Barbarians crawl, a history disappears,

So a soul's
Random misgivings can
Disappear, detach, for wishing on,

                  A single star.

              7

Complete their letter O they cannot,
             The sheer strakes, though
Hulls float, signs roll, cluster
             One by one, and point:

Only their being mirrored, mirrored being
             Can make a little fishing boat
Named Pure Ellipse, complete a melon segment,
             Say, untoothsome rind,

And find a globe. The mirrored boat, on zero,
             Surfaces, neither
Boat nor surface, but a canopy spread
             By the whirl of an *axis mundi*

Burnishes deep silence, bids midget words
             Dance in a last light
Where engines chug and loud all night on a roof
             There were seven voices,

Storms of laughter, stories, language,
             Rough-hewn, another bastion
Canopied the mirroring. Notions, move over:
             Those were the boatmen.

On a Photograph of Chekhov

for Katharina Wagenbach

While the rain comes pouring down,
Chekhov, in his white peaked hunting cap,
And prone beside a rick of hay, surveys
The scene behind the camera, narrow-eyed.

While in Berlin the rain comes pouring down
And will refresh the yellowed centenarian
Blossomer in the courtyard, Chekhov has
Anchored his umbrella, gone to earth.

Ivory handle of the slim umbrella shaft atilt
To birch trunks in the background, has a curve;
Eyesight arching clean across the image
Divines, in the cap's white crown, a twin to it.

Chekhov's brother, meanwhile, props his head –
Summer rain, phenomenally somber –
On Chekhov's hip; from his blubber mouth
A howl escapes, the sockets of his eyes

Are black, as if he wore, beneath his bowler,
Smoked eyeglasses; as if he were, perhaps,
A horror Chekhov carried on his back, and still
The rain comes pouring down, and the umbrella,

Hulk become a dome to shelter Chekhovs, both,
Can float across a century, be put to use.
O perishable hayrick! – and its fringe,
Where Chekhov tucks his knees up, will be damp.

Yet Chekhov's massive cap, laundered a day ago –
Intent beneath its peak his eyes are watching
How people make their gestures through the rain,
Set dishes on a table, turn

Vacant faces to the window, wring their hands,
Cling, so predisposed, to their fatal fictions,
Or stroke the living air, to make it hum
With all they mean to talk about today.

Egyptian in the Tube

The usual rumble of the doors
And at Swiss Cottage in she steps.
I should have seen, there and then, her face
Of golden bird, but it was plain
Until, a picture in my hands,
It flashed upon me, golden bird, at Finchley Road.

Yes, the toes a little splayed
Placed on the border of a Cretan rug –
Rose pyramids at first, but then
Cuneiform wedges, very red;
And up and up to the second foot, there
She put it, on a cushion, sat erect,
Capped in hair which glistens like
The plumage of a predator:

Enormous glance of eyes directed at
A mirror's back, intent, I mean the gaze,
Horus-Eye, it was the apex of
A triangle the fingers of one hand
Had mounted on a base
The other hand, her left, drew taut,

And knotted round her tiny waist she wears
An emerald, ordinary sweater trailing
Down across her danskins at the groin.
As if about to run, the glance, the poised
Seventeen-year-old and lithe
Presence, in a split
Second she'll release the arrow, yet
Spellbound she poses

Housed in a web of triangles crisscrossing
A rhomb that slopes the other way –
An ottoman festooned with rugs of wool,
Pink, to crescendo in the Cretan wedges.

She held the mirror for a cat
To see whatever, perched on fur,
A cat might see in a mirror:
All you saw was the cat's golden eyes,
They shot a horizontal to complete
Another triangle, for her hair is parted
Right above her nose, a line descends
To the spread-toe foot and ricochets
Off one toe's tip,
Past the other foot's contour,
And up to where the cat begins
To hump its back.

When I stood to leave, doors rumbling open
At Finchley Road, I saw no less marvel:
Opposite, Egyptian in the Tube, my neighbour,
There she was, one shoeless foot
Arched on the nondescript upholstery,
The other on the floor. Golden bird, she looked
Me up and down; I had become
The mirror in her hand; I was her cat.

We closed the book, and it was over.

More and More

More and more
In this day and age
I crave an old book;

Not one to collect,
More like the book
I saw being fingered
By a village idiot;

That was long ago,
And in Malaucène;
Fingering his book
He would come by;

For what was in it,
For his thought of it,
For the feel of its weight
He would finger it.

And so I wanted
A book like that;
But now the thought

Of the idiot's book
Has fashioned afresh
The actual idiot,
His particular book;

Craving has blent the two
Into one, the figure
Doubles back to a limit.
Still if I say

I want an old book
Then I am craving it still;
If the craving outwits me
Still I mean it:

I do not forget the book,
But opt to be the idiot.
Could it be, after all,

Only the moment I want,
Unreversible, gone,
At a café in Malaucène
A wobbly table, and Ann

(Her stars with mine aligned)
Nodding when our Anastase
Moseys past, all smiles,
With his fingering book?

Perhaps. Yet more and more
It is the real book now,
Fundamental enigmas glow
Pictured in it,

Inviolable, an old book,
A pulsing tomb of a book.
My desire has chosen

A book-to-be;
Shooting onward
And curling back
My desire would not stop

Even if I fingered
Its object, I suppose;
Even if it were there,
Now, the book, and solid,

My desire would still
Fan wildly out,
A ray of life, penetrating,
Springing every trap.

With all due respect
To the crystal worlds
And companies of concepts
That hem flesh in,

I would put first
This homing of desire
On the old book,

Which never was a book,
Though the book opens
When freely for a heartbeat
Spirit breathes again.

Some Dogs

Hereabouts there was a time of day
When the dogs came out of doors
Content to lie down in a garden.

Autumn's first cool, streets refreshed,
Flesh more than ever willing –
The clouds whiffed across the sky, so pink;

So blue the sky it was a cup of delphinium.
Somewhere else, poplars and olive trees
Were turning into a silver screen, so fast

People walking past them, with a scythe
Or sack across their shoulders, wore
Inexhaustible liquid outlines.

There too the dogs rested from their work.
Wild rabbits breathe again, gazing at space
In his café the old man mutters "fils de pute".

A gap in the bush gives you one more chance
Now, when the dog walks from his house,
To hear the breath expelled as his body meets

The ground, to see him crook a foreleg, fold
A paw to rest the back of it on earth, and tuck
The pad beneath his breastbone. He looks around,

One thought obliterating in that instant
Every single smell or sound in his neighbourhood:
My dish was full, now I have licked it clean.

The Parrot House on Bruton Street, 1830

This very young man, face all flesh and bone,
Eyeglasses, gold and owlish, perch between
Parrots he peers at and his jungle brain. Those eyes,
So myopic they must blink to capture,

Accurately, screaming parrots, one by one.
In a keeper's grip, wingtip to wingtip,
They measure such and such; he is making moues,
Surely he mimes the volumes of their hornblack beaks.

Then while a thieving pencil sweeps up the crests
And down his own bent backbone strokes the plumage,
Turquoise, into place, people tiptoe in, to watch
Our artist copy the parrot he all but becomes.

Odder far he thinks these wicker bonnets,
Eyeballs which are beads, gnawed snickering lips,
Than they have deemed his amiable psittacids;
And look, now he delineates the people's noses –

Upon my word, how sniffily those humbugs behold
Not a "dirty artist" or "Wog's Robin" now,
But being tweaked, nothing to snicker at,
The organs of their own inquisitivities.

The Lime Tree

Thank you for giving birth to me in the first place,
Thank you for delivering me from the dark,

You whose round arms I stroked with feeling
Made presence atmosphere and contact known.

And I wanted not that Englishness;
I wanted deliverance from you so soon,

From the sticky stuff you weltered in,
Leaf, branch, and bole in your shade they dispensed

The glue, the fragrant glue, but your blossoms,
Lady, they did provide the pleasure of tea.

You stood in your own glue, fascinated,
Stirring soup, mothering lambs, telling your sex

318

Hush, don't you bother too much about it;
It, it, the enormous poison tree, once fire,

In your conscience you capped it off, mere fume;
In hope that hurt might never occur, defensive,

You dreamed of hoopoes perching in your crown,
Drenched in your glue for ever their crests of rose:

So the maternal shadow works mischief with men;
Their quarrels rumble first in the glue cocoon.

Now you sleep, sag-jawed, in your wing chair,
Doped, breathing steady, life will not let you go:

You who could see the colours in every back street,
Who told the stories, magnifying into marvels,

Detail on detail, the turns and twists
Of happenings that never were not nice –

Game old chattel who never peeped over the rim,
Who less than once in a blue moon could scream

Uncongealing, suddenly rid of the stuff
Your civilization spurted over you, glue

Twinkly as the round of talk you spread,
Lawn sprinkler, swivelling over shorn

Tips of grass blades, while our wrinkled lips
Sip tea in the bosque it cools.

For sure this line is not easy, but it must out:
Lime tree, your fragrance called me, always

Tenderly, back, but on, on I had to go, not
Looking for anything, but at every thing for the sign

That flashes up-down, lightning bolt, a blade
Cleaving the creatures, glued from crisp.

I was for the owls, for hornets, for nomads,
For such fools as never knew they were honest,

Who have wandered far, to come through,
Who have bitten their way through,

Who have learned what it means to be altogether
Alive, unattached. Of nippled hard

Breasts to be sucked, of glue
Twixt lustrous thighs, of moisture

In the mouths of girls I did not speak,
For it is all glue. What now am I on about?

Who? A creature who cares to come by,
A silvery one, brisk, with her own story:

Sixteen, with a child who walks before her,
While in and out through quick disguises

She who shimmers has to slip.
"See this headband?" A motto on it.

"Now you read it," and I could, it said:
"Not one day's help from anyone."

Here she shimmers mercy through my thick sleep,
Gives me her hand, and it is flesh,

Looks at me, leaves me, with what her look can give
She lifts the glue, all of it, out of me.

Naked Truth

What I really wanted to say, I could not:
Animals wear their clothes all the time.

Waking up in the night I find the cat
Has woken up less than a breath before.

So he was waiting to go out into the dark;
He knew the exact moment I would let him.

There are things he knows by his silence.
If he meows it is because he knows

A person expects of him some kind of speech.
Among cats he will only hiss and spit,

And he keeps to himself the purr to relieve
And grasp, one breath at a time, his servitude.

When one front paw lifts, the other three pick up
The tremble of labyrinths alert in other rooms.

What beckons other cats out from behind walls?
It is their sinews hearing those three receivers.

So air in a painting links acrobats or bottles.
So silence walks in the connected fashion of cats.

There are things he knows by his silence;
I would like to speak in his clothes.

Postscript to Selected Poems

The selection differs somewhat from the ones in my *111 Poems* (1983) and in *Selected Writings* (1989). It spans the years (as regards writing) from 1957 to 1995, and it is drawn from eight books published between 1962 (*Torse 3*) and 1996 (*Intimate Chronicles*). The sequence matches, more or less, that in which poems appeared in those books; but in each book the poems were arranged in a definite pattern, not chronologically, and not randomly.

Details in some poems being abstruse, the following notes might explain extrinsic factors that gave rise to them:

'Climbing a Pebble': Nares and Keats refer to Robert Nares, *A Glossary or Collection of Words, Phrases, Names, and Allusions to Customs, Proverbs, etc.* (...) *in The Works of English Authors* (...), 1876; and to a late letter from Keats describing a sight he enjoyed near Rome.

'Five Psalms': The epigraph comes from Camus' *L'étranger.*

'January 1919': Karl Liebknecht, German Pacifist and Communist leader imprisoned during World War I, was re-arrested in 1919 and then shot "while attempting to escape". John Heartfield mounted a photo of his head on the cover of *Dada-Almanach*, 1920.

'Sanity': the title is the name of the newspaper issued by the Campaign for Nuclear Disarmament in the 1950s and 1960s.

'Merope': the title gives the name of the sweetheart of Sisyphus (his fate in the myth overshadowed hers).

'Found Poem with Grafts': a French-English conversation manual of 1866 provided the main text; the grafts allude to Cézanne and his muddy paintings of that time in Paris.

'In Balthazar's Village': Balthazar (better known as one of the Three Kings of Orient) is the patron of Le Barroux, in 1969 still a humble village in the Vaucluse.

'Opoponax': The name is that of an ancient Mediterranean perfume; the poem has to do with the planting and harvesting of lavender.

'On Mozart's Birthday': Osip refers to Osip Mandelstam, one of his images, and his death in banishment.

'Caromb, Vaucluse': In the village of Caromb, near Carpentras, there used to be a home for mentally handicapped children. "For" can be read to mean "on behalf of" as well as "addressed to".

'Jacob's Hat': Refers to the painting by Delacroix in the church of St. Sulpice, Paris.

'In Anatolia': The poem was written, largely in monosyllables, for a Japanese schoolgirl glimpsed in a Texas restaurant.

'A Pinwheel': The arrowhead belonged to Joseph Brodsky, the wooden cup to Cecil Collins. Internal rhymes for the pleasure of the rhymophiliac Brodsky.

'Cabaret de la Canne, January 1855': Monologue for Gérard de Nerval on the eve of his suicide. Alfred Delvau described such a meeting with him.

'Night Wedding in Anamur': I witnessed the wedding dance, at which the bride, at first, resembled a corpse, perhaps in accord with ancient folk tradition. Anamur is on the Turkish Mediterranean coast.

'Egyptian in the Tube': The painting alluded to is Balthus' 'Le

Chat au Miroir III', 1989–1994, of which a reproduction, as I was reading about it, faced the girl sitting opposite in the London Underground.

'The Parrot House' refers to Edward Lear at one of his early occupations.

Index of First Lines

Index of Titles

330